HOW TO ANALYZE PEOPLE:

Psychology Facts You Should Know For The Best Results In Mind Hacking Process, Learn How To Read Facial Expressions And Body Language On Sight. The Ultimate Guide!

Jack Carter

CONTENTS

INTRODUCTION

Before we consider some of the methods that you can use for persuasion and analyzing others, we first need to take a look at some of the steps that you can take to get a close look at the way humans behave. When we think about human behavior and some of the things that you need to do to read these behaviors, it is vital to take a look at the animal element that is found inside.

While this is something that a lot of people are going to forget about, humans are from the same materials like trees, animals, fish, and everything else in the world. We all came from the same source at the same time. Much of our behavior is going to be attributed back to our evolution. As we changed over the years, we started to develop what is known as cultural norms for the behavior that we are going to show to others.

Over time, we had to develop systems of behavior and specific patterns to help us survive. This means that in the beginning, we had to be able to hunt and gather. And then, we had to form systems for farming, along with other food systems. This continued to grow into the system that we have today. Just like with any other animal, we are going to have different behaviors, ones that are used to protect us, to eat, to sleep, to interact with others, and so much more.

This is something that we need to keep in mind when we are learning more about the behavior of humans. It isn't enough to consider the conscious state of the person when you want to understand the reasons they do things. We also have to remember that animal sense, the part that helps us survive, as well. We have to remember that this animal part is going to drive us towards specific actions, especially when things like self-protection, pleasure, food, shelter, and even sex drive the actions. This is where all of our basic drives come from, even if they happen subconsciously.

The first area, the one that is the most accessible, is the conscious. This part is going to be the most accessible and the things we know about and our current thoughts, but it is also going to be known as the smallest of the three parts of our psyche.

Then, we move on to the second part of our psyche, and this is going to be the subconscious. This is going to be an area that is more repressed when compared to the first part, but we can still access it, especially when it is the most needed.

Then, we have the third part. This part can be called the id or the unconscious. This is where all of those animal-like impulses are going to come in. These help us to survive and get our most basic needs met regularly. The id is not going to be something that we are in control of, or that we have to focus on that much. But, it can still drive a lot of our regular actions.

This will tell us a lot about the behavior that we can observe in those around us. There are going to be a lot of deep underlying factors that come with our behaviors, and it can be challenging to determine the cause of those actions. You can also guess what is causing the actions, and there are even some experiments that you can use to pinpoint what is causing these actions.

One of the proponents who wanted to use science to help us understand the human behavior that seemed hard to follow in the past is B.F. Skinner. Skinner was one of the most influential psychologists of the 20th century. He was the one who developed the ideas of behaviorism along with the school of psychology that is going to focus the most on measurable and observable behavior.

Firstly, behaviorism is going to be one of the schools of psychology, one that is going to be focused on science and will emphasize just looking at the measurable data that we can explore about the behavior. When you use this school of thought, you need to try to focus on not letting qualitative judgments get in the way of the science that comes in here. Over the years, it has proven to be one of the most influential schools of thought in all of science history.

What these schools of thought are going to do is try to make some sense out of our evolutionary history as a species. This means we are going to take a look at why we are the way that we are. Going by an evolutionary approach is going to be vital because it allows us to look at some of the best mysteries of how the human mind works. In an evolutionary sense, we are going to be driven to self-protection, a need for food and shelter, and so on. These are often going to be an unconscious part of our lives now, but it is still a good idea to explore this a bit and understand how some of these basic instincts are going to come into play.

For example, the feeling of anxiety is going to be a significant byproduct that is still left from our past. Our ancestor was always under worry about how they were going to survive. They had to fight off other animals, worry about their health, find food, and even worry about the weather. The world they lived in was not very secure and safe, and so they had to deal with a lot of anxiety to get through it.

Humans are always going to be driven naturally to try and protect themselves, and in many cases, this is going to take the form of an anxiety response. This response is going to mean that they go with fight or flight and that the blood starts to pump, the breath gets faster, and they begin to feel a bit scared or fearful.

This may have made a lot of sense to us in the past. This is the way that we were able to survive. But, when we move into our modern day lives, we know that we no longer need to protect ourselves from nature, from not having food, or from big animals any longer. We may need the same physical protection in some cases, but these situations are not going to happen all often, and most of the time, the negative parts of our anxiety response will outweigh the benefits when we are in this state.

This is going to bring up the next topic that we need to explore. We must remember that repression is going to play a significant role in our behavior. Many of the behaviors that we carry around naturally will be repressed. This may help us to live through our cultural norms today, but it means that these behaviors are going to have lots of time to build up. And several outcomes can show up.

Sometimes, the person who has the repressed material will never let these out, and it will stay hidden away in their subconscious forever. And then, it is also possible for this to manifest in behaviors that are not healthy, such as ones that are considered risky or addictions. Almost always, some pathology will show up, and it is going to show up in the different behaviors that we do decide to show off.

One of the aspects of understanding humans behavior that we often forgot about is that we need to understand the context of the behavior and where it happens. Someone's behavior in an untouched, native land is going to be much different than someone who lives in Iceland, and this is different from what we see with those who live in Mexico. Different areas of the world and various cultures are going to interact and do things differently than others.

Of course, even across the world, there are going to be a few similarities that we all share. For example, pretty much anywhere you go in the world, the culture is going to have some funeral procession or a way to respect and bury the dead. Many cultures are going to have some music, and it is going to change based on what it wants to show off, such as sadness, war, and celebration. Most cultures are going to have their ways of dealing with grief, even if this method is different based on the culture.

Even though some similarities are going to show up in the way we express things. For example, in Montana on a rural ranch, there could be an excellent culture for raising livestock and riding horses.

The children who are growing up in this family will be able to learn their duties should be fulfilled, and they are going to have certain expectations on them about how they need to behave, and what role they have in life. They are then going to see this as normal and how they are supposed to live their lives.

However, there can be a different kind of normal for a different family. If you find a child who is growing up in the Spanish Harlem neighborhood in Manhattan, their experience growing up is going to be a lot different than the child, who came from Montana. The family is going to have a different role in the community, and the culture is going to be different.

This is something super important when it comes to being able to analyze the behavior of humans around you. There is no right or wrong culture, just differences based on where they grew up and what was considered necessary at that time. The way that one person deals with grief is going to be different compared to what another person does. And this is true with how they deal with anger, sorrow, happiness, and more.

The trick to this is that we need to understand how the behaviors surround all of the different events and situations. And to do this, we need to figure out what the other person thinks is normal for them. This could easily be different than what you see as being normal. Think about where the person is from, how they raised them, and then take this into account when figuring out the way that the person reacts, and the way that they should.

Being able to take a closer look at how someone is going to react to certain situations is going to make a big difference in whether you can understand them and read them. If they are from a completely different area than you, or who came from different families than you, then it is time to consider this before you start to judge or look closely at the body language and behaviors that they are showing to you.

Taking into account the context of the behavior and actions that you use takes a lot of knowledge of the area and the history of your location right now, and where the other person is from as well. For example, if you talk to someone else who says that they are from a small town in upstate NY, and you have never been to that area, then it is not a good idea to make some bad generalizations about that person. Because you think that them being from a smaller town, they are uncultured and won't understand you.

Instead of doing this, and losing out on the connection that you want to earn with them, you should spend more time asking them about their hometown and trying to learn a bit more about that place and what it is like. This helps you to gain a better understanding of that person and how you will be able to connect with them and read them later on.

It is hard to analyze the person you are near if you assume that everyone is just like you, or you make some assumptions about that person that is not that accurate at all. And if you are not willing to learn more about them, put their actions into context, and pay attention, then you may as well give up now. Let go of the assumptions and the preconceived notions that you have, and instead, focus on learning about that person. This is the best way that you can connect with that other person and get them to open up to you and be open to your persuasion later on.

The next thing that we need to focus on is how we can analyze, and even decipher, the different behavioral patterns of those around you. Behaviorism is going to require that you only take a look at the things that you can observe. What is observable is mostly going to be the actions that you can see. Sure, sometimes, when you can see the emotions of the other person based on what comes out on their faces and body, but usually, the only thing that we can observe are the actions.

The neat thing here is that we also can talk to the other person and ask them about their behavior. We can then base our research on the answers to these questions. For example, you could talk to someone and ask them to rate out how they are feeling today on a scale from one to ten. Or you can ask a thousand people what they consider their favorite food. The response is going to be able to give you some of the information and the data that is needed to experiment.

However, while you can ask the person about their actions in some cases, you will usually observe the behavior, and then glean the data that you can out of that. If you are training your cat to respond to a bell, for example, you will be able to count out how many times ringing the bell produces the result. This is an excellent framework to focus on that helps us to understand a bit more about how we can observe the patterns. This is going to be done by thinking about some of the reinforcement mechanisms.

These classic mechanisms are going to be used in our daily lives, even though they may sound complicated. They are going to be some of the best strategies to use to train others and yourself to act a certain way, and you can then use them to help you to analyze the behavior of those around you better.

So, to get started with this idea, we first need to get to work looking for what caused a particular behavior. Whether we are looking at the emotion of happiness, joy, excitement, sadness, anger, or more, you will be able to look around and see if you can find what caused the person to feel that behavior.

Body language is an excellent place to start. For the most part, this body language is not going to be something that can be taught. You can watch your parents and others and pay attention and grow up that way. But unless we spend time practicing our body language and learning how to use it the right way, this is going to be something that we do without thinking about it.

There are a few of these body language skills that we can learn how to use effectively, but often, it is going to be about tapping into some of the things that we already know, and what is already intuitive and natural for you. Analyzing these behavioral patterns can be done when you learn new skills, but a significant part of it is just going to be learning how to trust the things that you already know, and then tapping into the natural perception that is already inside of you.

WHY OBTAIN THE BEST RESULTS IN MIND HACKING PROCESS

Since you have got a lot of insights into reading other people's personality; let us tell you why you need to analyze people and what is the significance of it.

Importance of Analyzing

Analyzing means to examine or study something carefully in a methodical manner. If you analyze your children's report card, you may agree on their potency and weak point. In simple language, analyzing people is reading a person's current state of mind, body, and emotions through your eyes. Analyzing varies from individual to individual as every individual has different perception or outlook to observe a trait in an individual but the conclusion would more or less similar if conducted on an individual. There is no formula to analyze people around or with you. Some people understand on the basis of their gestures, body language, verbal communication, nonverbal communication or the way he walks and dresses up. It comprises of primarily-

Studying yourself

Understanding the nature of the person you are trying to analyze

scrutinizing his behavior

Focusing on the words of another person

Knowing body language

Getting acquainted with cultural difference

Concentrating on social skills

Forming a general assumption on the nature of a person

Interpretation of verbal communication and pattern

Knowing the reason behind his type of personality

Having an elementary overview of the personality of an individual

Importance Of Understanding People

Why is it important to understand a personality? If you are ambitious, then yes it is important to read the other person but if you do not want any growth professionally and happy with 9 am to 5 pm job then it is not your cup of tea. Likewise, if you value your relationships, analyzing folks is important. Analyzing people is of immense importance from the perspective of life more than any other realm like professionally.

More finely you understand yourself and other folks around, the more booming you will be in dealing with the circumstances and people and getting things on the right track. Understanding personalities is an unexpectedly comprehensive and practical subject than psychology. It is an extensive word comprising of psychology and implementing the analysis to day to day advantage in everyday circumstances. It is vital to stay with family and amongst friends as well as colleagues. Learn it, to be the best and different of all members of a group. Get it to attract people, to help, to support, to influence, to raise your voice and to express your point of view, to understand better, to make right and fast decision, to encourage people, to manage people, to direct folks, to solve the conflicts and most importantly to portray the right personality of ourselves.

Advantages Of Analyzing People

People are an open book needing little attention to understand their traits. On closely observing what they do, what they say and how they listen to others saying reveals a pretty good picture of their attitude and personality. It has proven to be effective and true in most of the cases. It is best that you can do as a friend, family member, colleague or a boss in the office. Analysis of people, their behavior, body language, and gesture is a fascinating phenomenon because of diverse learning experience based on traits or behavior adopted by a person. It is therefore significant and essential to be successful in distinct walks of life like a business arena, day to day life, companionships, relationships, etc.

Let us have a quick look at the advantage that results due to the analysis of people:

Analysis of people offers an individual the knowledge of skills required to deal with people. It mostly throws light on tips to conduct with positivity.

It assists to recognize, realize and uphold human life and its standpoint, thereby shun conflicts.

It helps an individual develop understanding and sympathy towards others and results in a reduction of people from getting judgmental and restricts the person from pointing the finger at others.

It fabricates a healthy society enabling people to evaluate themselves before judging others.

Every individual to succeed in life requires important interpersonal and communication skills to be able to stand at a pioneering position in the corporate sector as well as in society which is always changing. In today's time when students and people are migrating out for jobs and studies, the study of the analysis of people is quite handy to understand people abroad and to minimize the possibility of deception.

Study of people is a type of preparation tool to cope up with the colleagues at the office and work efficiently at work front as well as social life.

It aids in comprehending the presence of imperfection in their life which can be improved by understanding the behavior of the other person and following his good features.

We live in a society where people of different personalities, beliefs, attitudes, perceptions, and behaviors are found. Their analysis helps to get aware of the techniques to deal with them.

It can be immensely helpful for people at management level in picking up the right employees by understanding the behavior of their employees.

Through analysis, you can project, direct, alter and control the distinct behavior of an individual

Through analysis of people, you can get an idea of his reaction in a particular situation in advance and get prepared for the situation.

Analysis of people is helpful for the successful conduct of society and accomplishment of goals.

TIPS READY TO USE FOR READING BODY LANGUAGE

The same way you train a dog to listen to your body language and cues, you can train a human being to follow you without question. Now there are some people out there who would automatically say that blind obedience is a dangerous thing, this book is not for them. Rather, this book is for those who understand the potential benefits associated with a little absolute control and are willing to do what is required to make that dream a reality.

This won't happen automatically, of course, few things worth having are obtained easily after all, but with practice, you will be able to subtly exert your will on those around you for your own ends. The first step to control those around you lies in analyzing them, however, which is why this chapter will discuss how to analyze people based on their body language.

While initially, you might feel nervous, if you instead make a point of focusing on the body language of those around you and try to pinpoint what type of personality you are dealing with. You might notice the people around you are not exactly at ease, or perhaps some of the people around you seem to be beaming with confidence. You will watch and listen. It is time to train the dog.

Choleric: Generally speaking, you should be able to pick out any cholerics in the room as they are the ones who cannot sit still. If you hope to successfully influence this person, then you are going to need to be prepared to make up for their lack of patience. You can usually hear the choleric person before you see them which is a sign they are in a good mood. It does not take much to get this person's attention because they are happy to give it.

You may find that you have the most difficulty with this personality type as they tend to want to share their passions with others which means they are often naturally charismatic. They may even naturally dominate other personality types, especially phlegmatic individuals which means you are going to need to deal with them first if you are in a group setting. They tend to be natural planners which means they will go along with what you say if you present it as a logical solution to a specific problem.

Another dead giveaway that you are dealing with a choleric person is that they tend to be less emotional than the other personality types. This means they are more likely to be unsympathetic if you play to their emotions and are more likely to be inflexible in general. As such, you will need to appeal to their logic if you hope to make progress. You can use this lack of emotion to your advantage as well, however, as cholerics are often uncomfortable around excessive displays of emotion.

Phlegmatic: On the other side of the scale are the phlegmatic individuals as they are going to be the ones that seem to be the most content with whatever is currently taking place. They will likely be at ease with you or anyone else who approaches them, and you will need to match their wavelength in order to make positive headway with them. One of the best things about phlegmatics is that they are consistent which means that once you convince them to come around to your way of thinking, you won't have to worry about doing it again. They are also naturally affable and prefer to reconcile differences if possible. They are often shy, however, which means they may freeze up if you come at them directly.

Phlegmatic individuals tend to prefer stability to change which means they are often susceptible to ideas that involve remaining with the status quo. As such, if you are ever going to convince them to go against the grain you are going to need to move slowly and get them to understand that they really have no other options. Keep in mind that they can be passive aggressive and don't respond in kind, this is only a response to their dislike of change and is more of an automatic response than anything else.

These types of people often keep their emotions hidden and put forth a relaxed and easy-going façade, regardless of what is going on inside. As such, it is going to take some extra effort to crack their shell and learn how they are really feeling. You may want to engage them in broad conversation to see if you can get a sense of what makes them happy and what makes them angry. Moving forward without this bellwether can be dangerous as it will be difficult to know if they like what you are saying or are opposed to it. While they are often willing to compromise rather than make a scene, they are often quite selfish and will resent any concessions they have to make. Don't forget they have no problem holding grudges.

Melancholic: The melancholic people in the room are likely going to be the ones looking back at you as you look at them. They are the ones who are most likely to be wary of you right off the bat so before you deal with them it is important to plan for resistance. These individuals are often given to deep thought, while still being sensitive to the thoughts and wills of others. This can cause them to focus too much on the innate cruelty in the world which can easily lead to bouts of depression.

One useful trait that most melancholics share is a desire for perfection in all they do which makes them highly conscientious of others. This is directly at odds with the difficulty they often have relating to other people, as they often fail to live up to the melancholic's standards. They are typically very independent and prefer to do things for themselves rather than settling for less than they believe they deserve.

As such, the best way to ingratiate yourself to a melancholic is to appeal to the sense of self-worth that comes along to their perfectionism. If you can find something that allows you access to their ivory tower, then they will naturally be far more inclined to follow your lead; after all, you've proven you have taste. They also only tend to focus on one thing at a time, which means you may need to lead the conversation in order to ensure that it gets to where you need it to be.

Sanguine: Sanguine individuals are known to be charismatic, impulsive and, above all, pleasure-seeking. If you are at a social gathering, then the sanguine individuals will be the loudest ones in the room making friends with everyone else. These personality types often have difficulty following through on tasks, however, which means that a great way to ingratiate yourself to them is by helping them complete the things they totally mean to finish but have not yet gotten around to.

It is very difficult to embarrass a sanguine individual, as they are typically shameless by nature and are always certain that whatever they are doing is the right choice. They are also virtually endless wells of confidence which means you will never make any headway with them by trying to convince them that they have made a wrong move.

They tend to be very physical and enjoy personal contact which means that matching this desire is a great way to score bonus points right out of the gate. They are also naturally curious which means you can also hook them early by showing them something they have never seen before, or at least promising to. They also love to tell stories which means listening and commenting when appropriate is another great ingratiation technique.

The biggest weakness of sanguine individuals is that they tend to feel controlled by their circumstances. As such, if you can convince them that the best way out of the latest situation, they have found themselves in then they will likely go along with whatever it is you are suggesting without a second thought. If you are in a social situation you will want to get them on your side early as they will be more than happy to spread the news of how great you are to everyone else at the party.

What to do with this detail: Knowing the different personality types will help you read people to decide who they really are. From here, you can decide what technique will be needed to persuade them or relax them for your own purposes.

If the other party looks away and down, and then back up at you, take advantage of this opportunity to consider them more closely. This is a sign of vulnerability which means they trust you, so you are free to do with that trust what you may. This is often a good time to ask them about themselves or offer something personal to break the ice. Compliments are always a good choice as it is hard to dislike someone who has recently payed you a compliment.

Smile: The most important asset anyone has is their smile. A smile is a window to the soul. If you are walking down the street and someone gives you a genuine smile, it can change your day. That is the power you want to carry around with you. This is the gift of most sanguine personality types. They are cheerful on the outside and can easily make people laugh. Faking a smile is hard. The truth of any smile lies in the eyes. Pay careful attention to the lines that form when the cheeks rise as the evidence of a genuine smile forms.

If you ask someone to do something and they decline, smile anyway, they will feel bad for saying no. Depending on their actual reaction, say it again in a different way and in a cartoonish voice (humor), and follow up with a serious voice. Ask for the favor again by adding another smile. This is best used in social situations and is to be avoided at work. Unless you are super cool with your co-workers or if you are sure you are dealing with a sanguine personality.

If your co-worker or your boss display a dislike for emotions or seem impatient, you could be dealing with a choleric personality. You will need to make it seem like they are the leaders. You're pushing boundaries, but you don't want anyone to recognize this game. No matter how it ends, do not give too much of a reaction. If you are too happy, it could kill the vibe. The same is true if you are too upset, just smile. You will not be able to change your own personality type as the theory is that you were born that way. However, knowing more about yourself, you can control the display, or even master your weaknesses to have influence or get close enough to other people, that you may sincerely analyze them.

Negative personality cues

Now that you have a basic understanding of positive body language, let us look at the opportunity to dig into the negative cues often given by different personality types. Sometimes even the most trustworthy and genuine people can give off signals of distress through body cues, so it is important to take them with a grain of salt to avoid being misled.

If you find someone who is trying to discourage you, or they are judging you, it is likely that their personality is phlegmatic If the negativity you are picking up on is coming from someone who is demanding attention or seems phony, you are amidst a sanguine personality type. You want to know the difference and how to respond to either situation to achieve a goal. Whether it is to cheer someone up, so you can enjoy their company or perhaps you need to get away from someone who would seek to destroy your aura. Either way, practice makes perfect, and observing takes a lot of it.

Personal space: If someone moves away from you, this is often a sign that they believe you either did something wrong or you represent something negative to them. This mentality applies to all four of the personality types. It hurts to feel rejected. Instead of feeling sorry for yourself, move back into their realm if you want to change the vibe.

Your sanguine personality types will not move away from you. They like to be close to the person they are listening to. Do not let this throw you off. Insist that you are worth it. Don't say it, but simply adjust your posture to a very relaxed position. You can do this by pointing your feet at that person, smiling and either asking a question about their job or what city they are from. From here, still smiling, ask if they want to get some fresh air. You have now created an intimate moment with someone who wasn't so sure about you. Let your sanguine personality do a lot of the talking if they do walk out the door with you as there is a good chance they will take a walk with you because they are restless.

Defuse a negative situation: If you need to stay cool until you can make an exit in a tough situation, avoid smiling. This occurs where someone is giving the impression that they are unstable or unsafe. Although, they are likely to be sanguine personality which is also known for turning people off, try to distinguish if they are angry or actually going to zap you of your will to live. What you need to do is avoid staring at the person but to make a few seconds of eye contact and act like everything is fine. This is an extreme example, but if someone had a gun to your head, you do not want to freak out and cry. Rather, you would want to stay calm, cool, and collected. This is the strength of a phlegmatic personality type.

Crying and carrying on, would irritate the person and they might lose their cool and shoot you. This could happen if they are a choleric personality type, which has an extreme distaste for tears and is unsympathetic towards other in general. in intense situations as it tends to make people a little calmer and more likely to bend to your will.

Looking side to side: Whether in a social setting or a professional setting, whoever you are dealing with should not be looking side to side. This means they are uncomfortable or bored. Are they coming across as guarded? A melancholic personality type may seem guarded when they are truly just in their own world. If you are confronted with this situation, use the opportunity to display positive body language to gain control of the vibe.

TIPS READY TO USE FOR READING FACIAL EXPRESSIONS

Is it possible to know the personality of people by simply looking at their faces? Read on for more information. We already know the study of people's face, physiognomy, existed from the times of Aristotle who referred to this science that connects people's faces to their personality traits and characteristics.

While the popularity of physiognomy ebbed and flowed through the history of mankind, its modern version started its run after the American Revolution. A set of pocket guidebooks were published by a Swiss enthusiast. In these books, the author gave easy-to-follow and quick tips on how to read faces while on the move. These books became very popular and it was during this time that George Washington's huge nose became popular as being reflective of his powerful inner personality.

Facial profiling has become very popular today and there are technology companies set up who create software which can profile a person based on his or her facial features. Yes, it may sound a bit weird but there are technologies like this available and used by law enforcement agencies all over the world.

Before we go into the aspect of how these law enforcement agencies use the rather path-breaking technology, let us understand the theory behind facial profiling. The software and hardware needed to do profiling of the face is not simple and consists of many complex layers and experts from various fields including those in facial analysis, computer vision, psychology, machine learning, marketing, and technology come together to create something tangible and useful for society.

So, why is facial profiling technology useful? These elements facilitate our ability to make improved choices about the person sitting in front of you physically or if you are seeing the individual on a computer screen.

Additionally, the face reveals the personality traits of the person. Taking into consideration the huge growth in the use of social media platforms, video cameras, and smartphones, pictures and images are freely available everywhere for facial profiling companies to employ and check out the veracity of the technology they are building.

Reading and analyzing faces accurately are extremely useful elements in making the right decisions about people and improve our own communication with them effectively based on first impressions. Facial profiling technology can affect the working and growth of multiple industries helping in the identification of:

- An effective academic researcher

- A professional poker player

- Extroverts and introverts

- White-collared criminals like pedophiles and others who manage to commit crime and get away

In fact, this kind of facial profiling technologies can be very useful in solving crimes and it is believed that security agencies across the world are keen on working with the companies that develop them.

THE THEORY BEHIND FACIAL PROFILING

Facial profiling technologies are based on the assumption that our face reflects our true personality in the following ways:

- Life science and social science studies have been able to prove that our personalities are affected by our genes

- Our faces reflect what we carry in our DNA

There are multiple research studies conducted by life science experts that reveal our genetic composition makes us who we are more than our external upbringing and other factors that surround us during our growth phase. These studies were done on a number of twins who were asked different kinds of questions such as:

- Are you happy with your achievements in life?

- Do strong opinioned people affect you and your opinions?

By analyzing answers to these kinds of personality-based questions, the research studies were able to reveal our genetic makeup is far more influential on our personality types than our upbringing and social conditioning and other such external factors. It was possible to prove that identical twins sharing the same DNA came up with very similar answers and their personality trait matched far more than non-identical twins. Psychologists also opined that the more powerful the genetic connection the stronger the family traits are carried forward.

Other studies which tried to connect genetic makeup with facial features were also proved to be right. Three of five genes were found to have contributed to how the face of an individual is formed. Therefore, it is quite clear that genes influence the way our faces turn out!

CURRENT USES OF FACIAL MAPPING TECHNOLOGIES

Facial mapping or profiling, as already explained has been happening for a long time now, and thanks to the computing power available today, it has reached new heights. Imagine having access to computing software that can use the features on your face and tell you what kind of a person you are. Recently, there have been instances when a facial profiling technology of an upcoming firm was able to predict 2 of the 3 winners in an international-level poker game.

Facial mapping technologies are also used to find out personality types and traits too. Recruiters can embed the software into their applications. Using images from real-time or video or camera recorders, the software will be able to return a score that reflects the confidence level and suitability of the candidate for the job applied.

Using facial mapping technologies, it is also possible to analyze faces from social media platforms and traffic cameras to arrive at the personality type of the individual concerned. Facial mapping uses the Big 5 Personality Test referred to as OCEAN, an acronym standing for Openness, Contentiousness, Extroversion, Agreeableness, and Neuroticism. These big 5 personality points are identified on your face as follows:

Openness

A person rated high on the element of openness means he or she is a curious and open-minded individual ready to check out new experiences and new knowledge. They are always talking in the following voices:

- I am imaginative

- I love adventure

- I love to try new activities and new realms of learning

Such a person's image will have the following characteristics:

- A facial expression that is neutral

- Such people tend to wear glasses as a symbol of their intellectual outlook

- 'Open' people usually give close-up shots and come closer to the camera lens

- As they are quite innovative and artistic, they deliberately stay away from any kind blur and colorful/natural tones so as to call attention on their picture

- They usually lean towards saturated, sharper, and high-contrasted colors

Conscientiousness

A highly conscientiousness person is described as highly dependable, organized, and efficient. People who get a high 'conscientiousness' score talk in the following voices:

- I am highly self-disciplined

- I come prepared and am very organized

- I prefer having a plan ready rather than being spontaneous

Such a person's image will have the following characteristics:

- Such people's images always sport a smile

- They prefer a smaller face ratio than those rated high on openness. Their faces usually back away from the camera lens

- There is a lot of color and brightness in their images

- They stay away from sharp, high-contrasted, and saturated colors

Extroversion

An individual with a high 'extroversion' rated is described as very outgoing and energetic. They speak mostly in the following voices:

- I bring life to any party

- I love being the center of attraction

- I enjoy starting a conversation with anyone

Such a person's image will have the following characteristics:

- His or her face will be like a beacon of light and there will be a huge smile most of the time

- The person will stay away from the lens of camera preferring a smaller face ratio so that more friends can be added

- There will be plenty of color and brightness too

Agreeableness

A person with a high 'agreeableness' rating is compassionate and friendly aligning with voices like:

- I am quite trusting of people and don't mind giving the benefit of doubt when there is a conflict

- It is easy for me to feel empathy

- I take a lot of effort to make others feel at ease

Such a person's image will have the following characteristics:

- Nearly all the pictures of such people have a hearty, smiling face

- The image will be bright and lively

- Such people like to have a bit blur on the sides of their pictures

Neuroticism

An individual with a high rating in neuroticism is usually quite a stressful being, always worrying a lot. They are nervous a lot of the time and they talk in the following voices:

- I feel so stressed out

- I am moody

- I worry a lot

Such a person's image will have the following characteristics:

- The pictures of these people are quite similar to the people with a high rating of 'openness' with a neutral expression on their face most of the time

- Plenty of negative emotions on display

- They wear glasses so as to appear as an introvert

- They get personal and up-close to the camera lens

- They stay away from blur and colorful or natural tones

- They lean more toward saturated and sharp colors

So, the answer to the question that we started this chapter with is a resounding 'Yes.' A facial profiling technology will be able to discern and clearly articulate the various expressions on the face and create a profile that matches the individual's personality. Although it is not a perfect science and a lot of work still needs to be done in that direction, the fact that such technologies can be very useful in the modern world is highly irrefutable.

Yes, like most things in the world, facial profiling also has its share of controversies and limitations. Let's look at some of them.

LIMITATIONS OF THE FACIAL MAPPING TECHNOLOGY

First, all technologies need data input and training for things to happen correctly. While artificial intelligence is an integral part of the modern-day facial mapping technology, it still is not human, and it is as intelligent as what is fed in and trained on. The images the technology will be able to analyze will be only those which it has been trained on and for which analytical data is available to the machine.

Additionally, accentuated facial features do run the risk of being misread and wrongly analyzed by the technology. If data is not constantly updated, then too, the chances of inconclusive readings or wrong readings are possible.

Moreover, these technologies may not have the perfection to handle differences in images such as those taking place because of weight gain or loss of the same person resulting in erroneous conclusions.

Another example of how artificial intelligence can go wrong is the following experiment: a computer was trained using data inputs and commands to identify differences between wolves and dogs. All the test results were 100% accurate. However, on further scrutiny, it was found that the computer took into account snow in the background to identify wolves whereas those images without snow were identified as dogs. The data input given to the computer had snow in the background in all the wolves' images whereas none of the dog images had snow. So, without the discerning mark of background snow, the computer will not be able to tell the difference between a wolf and a dog.

In addition to limitations, again like most things in the world, such powerful technologies can be misused by the people. It is an old age that goes a system is as good and moral as the people running it. Here are some controversial ideas that could go wrong with this technology.

CONTROVERSIES SURROUNDING THESE TECHNOLOGIES

We all have a face and it is easy to see that just like fingerprints, faces are unique to the individual and even with identical twins, it is possible to discern differences. This is the primary reason why facial recognition is slowly gaining popularity as a biometric modality as well. Face recognition and face profiling techniques can be misused by law enforcement agencies and other regulatory authorities to even frame and harass innocent citizens, claim opponents of this system.

There are a lot of stories in the media wherein the government agencies are picking up images from cameras put at traffic lights and other public places and using them to profile people even without the approval and/or knowledge of the person concerned. Facial technology can be easily misused if given to the wrong set of people.

There are studies which refute the correctness of facial profiling. While proponents want to make use of it to preempt crime and prevent it happening, especially of the large-scale terrorism-types, opponents opine that there is something called an "Othello Error" that can easily mislead the observer or maker of these facial profiles. The "Othello Error" occurs when a suspicious observer or profiler discount the visible truthful elements available in the scene so as to conform to his or her suspicions, which could be a deception too. This happening is common when the profiler is already under the impression that the person under the scanner is a liar. The former forgets that it is possible that the latter was compelled to lie under duress or anyone under stress can come across as lying.

Studies also suggest that subconsciously we human beings ascertain aggression in people based on their faces and their facial structure. Psychologists believe that subconsciously human beings read aggression based on a specific measurement of the face referred to as width-to-height ratio (WHR ration). Some studies proved that this natural ability to connect the WHR ration to aggression is also quite accurate.

Volunteers who participated in this study were able to discern aggressive men and also to determine the degree of aggression remarkably accurately. WHR is a number got by dividing the distance between the right and left cheeks with the distance between the upper lip and the mid brow of a person. Researchers observed that men with large WHR numbers were seen as aggressive and the greater the number the more aggressive the person was.

Yet, history has proved that physiognomy is not a perfect science and there could be mistakes made during the process of facial profiling. There are many instances where captured gunmen and proven murderers have not really got the 'criminal' profile. Take for example, the lone surviving gunman in the Mumbai terror attacks, Akmal Kasab. When the Indian police found him, they were in for a big surprise.

Here was a man who mowed down dozens of innocent people and he was just over 5 feet tall with the chubby face of a baby, which earned the sobriquet in the Indian media as the 'baby-faced killer'. The sight of this innocent looking face created panic among the Indians and they all started wondering whether he was the innocent victim of a warped society or was he a really dangerous killer.

Although the study of physiognomy has been around since ancient times, there are people who believe it to be nothing but an age-old prejudice and a loophole in our system of jurisprudence to harass the innocent without any concrete proof or evidence of guilt.

There is plenty of evidence in history in support of these opponents' scorn too. During the 19th century, Cesare Lombroso, a criminologist from Italy did autopsies on dead convicts and recorded and cataloged facial features of 'born criminals'. Some of these features included overdeveloped canines and jug ears. Similarly, in the early 20th century, a professor from Harvard, Ernest Hooton examined and recorded facial features of 14,000 criminals and using these recordings, he came to the conclusion that first-degree murderers usually have straight hair while second-degree murderers tend to have abnormally golden hair.

After some years, another Columbian psychologist, William Sheldon carried out a study on delinquent youth and cataloged them into different types including thin-faced, broad-faced, round-faced, etc. He claimed that the meaty faced youth were more likely to be criminals than the thin-faced ones. Under scrutiny, many of these studies and observations fell through large gaping holes.

CURRENT STUDIES ON PHYSIOGNOMY

Today, physiognomy is back with a bang, supported by tremendous growth in 3-D modeling and various kinds of advanced animation software. Combining with this, are older learning from evolutionary psychology and genetics which are helping people understand and analyze facial features far more accurately than before.

New physiognomists are able to revive older studies and see how they can cover the gaping holes and redo some of the categorizations in a better and more scientific than done previously. Studies at Princeton are proving that it will become possible for 5-year-olds to predict outcomes of elections based on photos of candidates! Far-fetched, yes, but anything is possible.

Studies at some other universities are revealing that it is possible for undergraduate students to gauge the aggression in a person by only viewing the face. Even the neck was obscured from view. These studies seem to point out to the fact that big and fleshy men were more prone to violence than the thinner and less fleshy ones. Scientists are even comparing this attitude to those shown in the animal kingdom.

Male orangutans are known to grow fat cheek pads reflecting their higher position in the pack. Similarly, lions with dark and long manes usually are the leaders of their pride. These facial features work like evolutionary advertisements that tell everyone around loud and clear as to who is the leader. So, big features seem to hint at some sort of belligerence.

Yet, everyone does agree that there are worrying gaps with regard to the accuracy of results observed through these facial mapping systems. Even CEOs of companies engaged in this business agree that the maximum accuracy possible is 80% and that 20% gap is worrying. However, they are quick to point out that these gaps can be easily filled by other technologies, people skills, facts and data during the process of face profiling.

ERRORS IN FACIAL PROFILING COULD SAVE LIVES

Let us look at the aspect of why we as a human race to overestimate the danger while seeing the face of an aggressive-looking person. This attitude is actually based on how our ancestors evolved. Survival instinct is an inborn trait in all living beings. All life forms are always looking out for elements that could harm them in any way.

Being able to identify these harmful elements is very useful in two primary ways:

• It gives us an opportunity not to make a mistake which could cost us our lives

• Overestimating danger is cost-free. The maximum cost could be the potential loss of a good friend along with a few anxious moments before you realize (thankfully) that you had overestimated the danger.

Therefore, if there is some little chance that you could get attacked, it is better to err on the side of caution and overestimate the danger than not believe in your instincts. Errors in facial profiling especially at the individual level can save lives and prevent mishaps such as rape and other crimes against yourself. Learning to read and analyze faces to save yourself from danger should be adopted wholeheartedly without worrying about being too judgmental.

In a large society-kind of scenario, it does make sense to be aware of misuse of this technology to label the innocents merely based on their facial structure and shape. Technology is only as good as the people who use it. There are always two sides of a coin. Facial profiling technology can be used to prevent crimes and catch culprits and on the other side, can be misused to label people unfairly.

Yes, there could be fraudsters in this realm like all other aspects of humankind. Yet, there are many good things that facial profiling technologies offer which can be effectively used for the good of mankind helping in choosing the right candidate for a job, to understand how people are behaving in your relationships, to help preempt and prevent crimes, etc. So, it is imperative that all perspectives are taken into account before passing judgment one way or the other.

HOW TO READ OTHER PEOPLES

Getting deep into the merits and ethical problems of reading the minds of others can readily be rejected on the brief floor that it is not a progressive concept. It is also accurate, in a manner, because of the very competitive and merciless scenario that exists in every industry. Reading people's minds provides a ton of advantages, in reality. It is feasible, too, but the methods need to be employed continuously so that your findings are almost ideal. Some of these methods are being discussed here.

It is an agreed fact that, by observing a person's body language and eye movements, you can find out what the person is thinking. Reading the signals of body language and eye movements is a great skill, and if you master it, you can do a lot of things. Some people seem to have this skill, of course, but many of us do not pay attention to the signals coming from others through these things. If this skill is to be acquired, you should start paying more attention to these aspects.

Great way to read people's minds is to observe their movements in the eyes. Experts have found out that if a person is looking up and down to the left, he or she is trying to create an image. If a person looks up and right, you can construe that he or she is trying to remember a particular image.

Another point is that nervous people, or those who speak lies, won't look directly at your eyes. If the person is shy or timid, you can't even expect the person to look at you directly.

Confident people, on the other hand, keep their eye contact for a longer time. The same is true for lovers. You can also see what's brewing in people's minds by watching facial expressions.

Someone is trying to get close to you; they will respond positively as you get closer to them. They'll stay where they are, or they'll try to get a little closer. If you don't like getting closer to them, they're going to retreat a little or move away from the scene.

You talk to a person; if the person agrees with you, the knees will be pointed at you. On the contrary, if your knees are turned away from you, you may conclude that whatever you say is not acceptable to them.

Likewise, nervous or impatient people keep shifting their weight or moving their legs. If you see a person sitting across his or her legs, you can easily see that he or she is an easy-going person.

-The position of the head will also help you to determine what people are thinking. Tilted heads show that you have sympathy for them. A tilted head with a smile on his face shows that he or she is a playful person or can even be interpreted as a sign of flirting. If someone lowers his head while talking, you can be sure that he or she is trying to hide something.

-Some people are going to try to mirror your behavior. This shows they're interested in you and they're trying to make a relationship with you. You can make a few changes to your behavior to test this, and if they also try to imitate these changes, you can be sure that they are very much interested in you.

-You should also observe the movement of arms to read the mind of the person. If a person folds or crosses his or her arms around the chest, they will try to protect themselves from the influences of others. If they keep their legs wider with such crossed arms, they show their toughness. If your hands stay on your hips, you can conclude that they're getting impatient. By keeping their arms behind them, they show that they are not opposed to discussions.

You're not supposed to get obsessed with this aspect of reading others. If you're over-zealous, others will find out that you're trying to figure out what they think or try to read. They're going to be a little rigid with you. This could damage your relationship with people. So, while you try to read people, you should take a subtle approach.

ANALYZING PEOPLE IN DATING AND LOVE

Jim is a lady's man. He exudes a masculine charm and smooth way of communication that other men would kill for. He can attend a social gathering and have the woman of his choice.

On the other hand, Jane is every man's dream of a perfect woman. She is not the most pretty or well-dressed. But she exudes a feminine charm that draws men in. It is easy for her to get any date of her choice while others find it difficult to get the man they desire.

As you can see from the above illustrations, Jim and Jane are living the life in terms of dating and courtship. They don't have to work hard to get the partner of their choice.

They may not be movie-star attractive, but they always seem to get lucky with their choices. So, what makes the difference between them and those who fail in dating?

You will get the answer to this question and learn how to analyze people in love and dating in this section. You will also learn how to properly use these attraction methods to attract who you want. I will also show you how to understand the physiological changes that take place when you encounter the opposite sex.

What Happens When You Meet The Opposite Sex?

According to Dr. Albert Scheflen, a renowned body language expert and the author of Body Language and the Social Order, there are different physiological changes that occur in the body when you come across the opposite sex.

For instance, a man walking toward a woman will strut out his chest in lieu of a slouched position, stand taller, and increase his muscle tone in preparation for the encounter.

On the other hand, a woman who's interested will push out her chest to increase her breast size, touch her hair, walk livelier, expose her wrists, and appear submissive.

You can see the different physiological changes that took place as they walked toward each other.

Body language is undoubtedly one of the fundamental components of dating, and it reveals how ready, desperate, insecure, confident, sexy, attractive, or available we are. Some of these dating body language responses are learned while some are completely out of our control.

Those who are the most successful at dating have realized how to optimize their body language to create an aura of attraction.

Why Jim And Jane Are Successful

Research on animal courtship behaviors by zoologists reveals that female and male animals utilize a series of courtship behaviors, some of which are subtle while others are obvious, with a large percentage of courtship behaviors done unconsciously.

For example, in many species of birds, the male puffs up his feathers and struts around the female while giving a vocal display to gain her attention. While the male performs his courtship behavior, the female shows little to no interest. This courtship behavior is similar to that performed by humans when dating begins.

Jim and Jane were able to perform a series of gestures that attracted the opposite sex. What's more? They were able to emphasize their sexual differences in order to look attractive to the opposite sex.

The secret of Jim's technique was to first stop women whose body language screams that they are available and then to send his own masculine dating gestures. Interested females return the appropriate feminine signal, giving him the go-ahead to continue to the next phase.

Jim knew what to look for, and women would describe him as sexy, passionate, masculine, and humorous. More so, they will describe him as someone who makes them feel feminine. On the other hand, men would describe Jim as arrogant, boring, and insincere due to their reaction to his success with the ladies.

Women like Jane are successful in the dating game because they are able to send the right signals to men and to analyze those like Jim, who are able to send back the signals.

In dating and love, women are more perceptive in analyzing dating signals while men are generally blind to these signals.

It's A Woman's World

Women call the shots in dating. Although if you ask a man who usually makes the first move during courtship, he would say that men do.

Studies show that women are the imitators of dating signals about 90 percent of the time. Any man who walks across to chat with a woman has done so after receiving positive signals from the woman. If, however, a man walks toward a woman without receiving a green light, there's a lower chance of success unless the man in question is Brad Pitt.

The Stages Of Attraction

As mentioned earlier, women call the shots in dating or courtship.

Therefore, a large part of this chapter will be focused on women and the attraction signals they give off. So, let's go through the five stages of attraction that we all pass through when we meet an attractive person.

Stage 1: Making Eye Contact

A lady will make eye contact with someone she fancies, and she will hold it long enough for the man to notice. Then she holds his gaze for a few seconds before she turns away. Now she has the man's attention.

The man will keep watching her to see if she repeats the eye contact. A woman needs to repeat the eye contact at least three times before the average man realizes the significance of the message—most men are not perceptive. This eye contact is repeated several times, and it's the beginning of attraction and flirtation.

Stage 2: Smiling

Once she has the man's attention, she delivers one or more half-smiles that are intended to give the prospective date a green light. Sadly, many men are not responsive to the half-smiles, leaving the woman to think that he has no interest in her.

Stage 3: Preening

This is the next stage after the half-smiles, and it involves heightening sexual differences. At this point, the woman sits up straight to push out her breasts and crosses the ankles or legs to show off her legs. If she is standing, she tilts her head sideways toward one shoulder and tilts her hips to one side.

She plays with her hair as if she is grooming herself for the man. She may straighten her clothes or jewelry or even lick her lips to make them more inviting.

The man will respond by standing up straight, expanding the chest, and pulling the stomach in. Lastly, they point their feet toward each other to show acceptance and willingness to proceed to the next stage.

Stage 4: Talk

The man, at this point, takes the active role by walking toward the woman in an attempt to make small talk. He will attempt to break the ice by using clichés, such as "You look familiar. Have I seen you somewhere?"

Step 5: Initiating Touch

After the initial small talk and well-used clichés to break the ice, the woman will look for an opportunity to initiate a light touch on the arms, either unintentionally or otherwise. Take note of these light touches. A touch on the hand is more intimate than a touch on the arm. Men can also initiate the light touch.

Though it feels less intrusive when it's first initiated by the woman. The light touch is then repeated to see if the person is happy with the first touch and to make them aware that the first touch was not accidental. She can also initiate a handshake to fast-track the connection.

To many, these five stages of attraction may seem minute or even incidental, but they are of great significance at the beginning of every relationship. This chapter will explore the likely signals sent by both men and women during the five stages of attraction.

Mirror, Mirror, Who's The Fairest In The Land?

In the famous Disney fairy tale, we saw the witch/queen asking the mirror to show her who's the fairest in the land. Well, most of us are familiar with how the story turned. If not, go brush up on Snow White and the Seven Dwarves.

Why am I referring to a fairy tale in a chapter on how to analyze dating signals? The answer lies in the fact that you can use the mirroring signal to know if someone is interested in you or not. Just like the magic mirror in that fairy tale, we aim to see a glimpse of the truth, whether someone likes us or not.

When you are in the same emotional state as the other person, you tend to mirror or copy their posture. For instance, if the other person is in a sitting position with the legs crossed over another, you find yourself mirroring the person's posture as your connection grows deeper. This is why I refer to the mirroring signals as the sixth stage of attraction. Interestingly, you can mirror someone you are interested in even though the person is on the other side of the room. How awesome is that?

Common Female Dating Signals And Gestures

Let's face it: we all hate it when our advances are rebuffed, especially when there are so many people watching. So how can we effectively analyze these signals in order not to look like a fool at the end of the interaction? First, let's explore women's dating gestures before we proceed to the common dating signals men give off.

Lip Pouting and Wet Lips

A woman's face maintains childlike features throughout her early to young-adult phase i.e., no sharp angles as every part is filled with subcutaneous fat. Her face appears thicker, especially the lips, which is used to create a feminine aura to entice the opposite sex. Some women inject collagen into their lips to give a thicker and more luscious look.

To give an appearance of sexual invitation, they may wet the lips via the use of saliva or lip gloss. When a lady becomes sexually aroused, her breasts, lips, and genitals become redder and larger as they fill with blood. Therefore, the use of lip pouting or lip wetting through the use of cosmetics is a way to mimic the reddened lips of an aroused female.

The Hair Flick

This is usually the first display a woman will use when she meets someone she fancies. The hair flick involves flicking the hair away from the face or over the shoulders. It is a subtle way for a woman to show that she cares about how she looks to someone she fancies.

Short-haired women also use this gesture to create the same effect.

The Limp Wrist

The limp wrist gesture is a sign of submission and femininity. It is commonly used by women and gay men. Just like a bird would feign a broken wing to entice prey away from the nest, the limp wrist gestures attract attention.

What's more? It makes them more attractive to more dominant men.

Self-Touching

When a woman touches her body in a seductive way, she is consciously trying to spike the man's erotic desires by fueling his imagination. For instance, when she slowly strokes her neck, thighs, and the sides of her abdomen, she is sending a signal that the man might get to touch her in those places if he plays his card right.

Fondling a Cylindrical Object

When you are on a date with a lady and you observe that she repeatedly twirls her fingers around the stem of a wine glass, cigarette, or continuously removing and inserting a ring on her finger, then it's a sign of acceptance. This gesture signifies the possibility of intimacy after the date.

Exposed Wrists

When caught, thieves and guilty people will often raise their hands, exposing their wrists as a sign of surrender. You can also observe this gesture in interested women in courtship. An interested woman will expose the soft underside of her wrist to her date. Interestingly, as her interest grows, he will increase the rate at which she flashes her wrist. The palm also becomes visible as she assumes this posture.

Sideways Glance over Raised Shoulder

A woman will use the sideways glance over a raised shoulder to catch the attention of the man she fancies. In men, this gesture creates the sensation of being peeped at, and it spurs them on to make a move toward the woman. With partially dropped eyelids that speak of seduction, a woman will hold the man's gaze just enough for him to notice her, then she quickly turns away.

Rolling Hips

Due to childbearing functions, women have wider hips than men. This means that she has an accentuated roll that highlights her pelvic region when she walks. Since men can't replicate this gesture, it has become a powerful sexual difference signal that shows femininity. This gesture is one of the subtle female courtship signals, and it is used by models to advertise goods and services.

Placing the Handbag or Purse in Proximity

Men have always known that it is impolite to touch a woman's bag without any form of intimacy between them. A woman's handbag or purse is an extension of her personal space, and it's a good indication of interest if she places the bag close to you. If she finds him attractive, she might slowly fondle or caress the bag while talking to him. She can even ask to pass her the bag or retrieve an item from the bag for her. When you see these signs, it's a great sign that your date is going the right way. However, it is a sign of emotional distance if the bag is placed further from the date.

The Knee Point

This is what I refer to as the "green light" gesture. It is a sign of complete acceptance and relaxation if a woman tucks one leg under the other, which is pointed toward the person she finds interesting. The knee-point gesture takes the formality out of the conversation and gives the date a slight glimpse of the exposed thighs.

The Shoe Dangle

At this point, I would say that you have successfully gained her trust and acceptance. When a woman dangles her shoes on the end of one foot, it indicates a relaxed attitude. Sometimes, she might use the phallic effect of thrusting the foot in and out of the shoe to show she's interested and open to more conversation. Sadly enough, this action goes unnoticed to many men since they don't know how to analyze the gesture.

The Leg Twine

A woman's legs are a great selling point, especially if they are long, slender, and smooth. To show interest on a date, a woman might assume this sitting position by crossing one leg over the other. Mind you, this is different from the crossed-leg gesture that represents defensiveness. In the context, the leg-twine or crossed-leg gesture show acceptance and seduction.

Women use the leg-twine gesture to consciously draw attention to their thighs. According to Albert Scheflen, when one leg is tightly pressed against the other, it gives the appearance of high muscle tone, which is a condition the body assumes even when it's time for sexual performance.

Women also cross and uncross their legs slowly in front of a man and gently stroke her thighs to show readiness to be touched.

Common Male Dating Signals And Gestures

Men don't have as many dating signals or gestures in their repertoire. The male display generally revolves around shows of power, wealth, status, and masculinity.

This is unlike women who have a range of gestures in their arsenal.

In this section, we will explore most of the male gestures you are likely to see during dating. A majority of these gestures are centered on the crotch region. Other gestures include standing tall, tucking the stomach, and pushing out the chest to boost his male presence.

He will smoothen his collar, straighten his tie, touch his watch or cuff links, brush an imaginary lint off his shoulders, and rearrange his coat or shirt.

The Male-Crotch Obsession

As mentioned earlier, a man's sexual display centers on placing emphasis on the crotch region. For instance, the thumbs-on-belt gesture is an aggressive display that highlights the crotch. When he's leaning against a wall or in a sitting position, he may also spread his leg to reveal his crotch region. He may also turn his body and foot toward you and use an intimate gaze to catch a woman's attention for a long time.

The crotch display is also observed in primates, where the male exerts dominance by sitting with their legs wide open to reveal the male organ. In New Guinea, natives use the penis sheath to assert their dominance and to exude sex appeal to the opposite sex.

On the other hand, some men in Western culture employ the use of tight-fitting pants or Speedo to accentuate the outline of their male organs.

The crotch adjust is also a common male form of sexual display that revolves around adjusting or handling the crotch. You will notice this gesture a lot when young males get together to show machoism.

Removal of Glasses

This gesture is common to both sexes. It's usually one of the signs that the person is lowering their barriers around you. It's more of an invitation that you are hitting the right buttons in the conversation. If instead, the glasses are held up between you then it is a strong signal that the person is not really buying what you are saying.

Puts Anything in the Mouth

Sometimes done by men, this gesture is frequently used by women to indicate interest.

Rhythmic Function

Swinging leg, toe tapping, fingers drumming, or leg bouncing on the tip of the toe are all movements that indicate the person is uninterested, impatient, nervous, or bored with what you have to say.

Closed Hands and Clenched Fists

The closed fists mean the other person has shut you out completely. It's a precursor to an angry or aggressive tone or outburst.

HOW TO FAKE YOUR BODY LANGUAGE TO PERSUADE AND MANIPULATE

First things first, the word "manipulate" has quite a bad rap to it, but for the purpose of this section, I would like you to see that word in a different light. To help you see manipulation from a different perspective, consider the following examples:

Jack wants his friends to have a great evening at a party. He suddenly bumps into one of them, spilling their drink in the process. Jack smiles disarmingly and apologizes for the accident even though clearly it was the other person's fault. Both had a great evening.

Jill wants to make her work colleague look bad. She spreads negative rumors about the colleague. Eventually, the colleague gets to hear the rumors and feels sad and loses self-esteem.

In the first example, Jack manipulated his friend's feelings to make them feel better about a bad situation. In the second example, Jill manipulated her colleague's feelings to make them feel bad. The problem is not with the manipulation; instead, it is with the motive behind the manipulation.

Here's the message I am trying to get at from the above: to manipulate (in the context of this book) is to intentionally influence someone into changing their mind or behavior without any intent of causing harm to the other person. It is a mutually beneficial act— a win-win for all involved.

"Fake it till you make it!" is a cliché that people use to motivate others to believe in themselves. This also holds true for body language. When you assume a body posture or a physical position or an attitude that you would like to have, your brain immediately begins to release hormones that make you actually feel that way!

Now that you clearly understand what I mean by faking your body language in order to manipulate others to do as you want, let me share with you two quick tips on how to fake it until you get the result you desire. I recommend that you should make a handful of videos of your verbal presentations in different situations. They don't necessarily have to be lengthy videos. When you play back the videos, turn off the sound so that you only see your body movements, gestures, and facial expressions. Observe what your body is saying. Does it say exactly what you mean? Is there a way you can make it convey the message you intend in a clearer way?

Few minutes before a meeting (in a social or professional setting), take deep breaths. Be present and mindful of your environment. Ensure that you take your attention off the meeting or whatever the near future holds and focus your attention on your present moment. This is a mindfulness practice. Steady yourself with deeper breaths. Clench and unclench your fists to make sure they are not shaky. All this will help you to become calmer when you eventually get into the meeting, and it will make you become more aware of your gestures and body movements.

Now, let us consider some of the practical ways to fake your body language properly so that you appear confident and interested in someone or make others comfortable around you even when you are not in the least any of these things!

Faking Interest

It is easy for anyone to tell you, "Show interest even when you are not." The problem with this advice is that the average person (who doesn't know how to fake their body language) is likely to become robotic in doing this.

First of all, you need to understand that interest has a lot to do with the human attention span. And the normal human attention span doesn't last for long—at least not without some form of disinterest at some point or distraction. So, when you are faking interest in someone or something, here's how to do it.

You have to look like you are interested, but don't overdo it. Human beings don't have a 100% attention span to anything for a long time. So, when you show interest (or fake interest in other people), be sure to keep the show up for only about 70% of the time. Trying to fake interest in someone for longer periods will expose you as fake!

No one likes it when they are being "taken for a ride." Well, that is what it feels like when you want to get something from someone by faking interest in them. The poorest way to do this is by showing interest in someone just right before you ask them for a favor. For example, someone approaches you and offers you a compliment, and right after that, they go, "I was wondering if you could help me . . ." and they blurt out whatever it is they were really after. It doesn't take a genius to figure out that the earlier compliment given was not an honest one but a means to an end—the end, in this case, being the favor they want from you. So, if you want to compliment the person, that's fine, but make sure to give the compliment genuinely.

Discuss a variety of issues that will lead up to the favor you intend to ask. While this involves verbal communication, your body language throughout the interaction should show that you have a genuine interest in the issues or topics you talk about.

Making People Comfortable Around You

Closely linked to faking interest in people is learning how to make people comfortable being around you. If you can fake this successfully, you will be able to build a strong rapport with other people in a relatively short amount of time. Interestingly, while you may feel it is fake and unreal at the initial stages of using these techniques, with time, you will become so good at it that it no longer feels like faking. This is when you have moved from faking it to making it!

Mirroring: The Chameleon Effect
The chameleon effect is simply mirroring the other person's body language and speech pattern. Tuning yourself to reflect the other person back to themselves is a quick way to make them feel really comfortable around you and even like you in the process. When you mirror or mimic their sitting posture, tone of voice, gestures, body angle, expressions, and so on, you send an unconscious message to the other person that tells them you are like them in many ways. This makes them relax or let down their guard around you.

This technique may sound easy to use, but in real-life application, it can be the worst giveaway that you are simply faking if you don't know how to use it. It goes without saying that being obvious about mirroring or copying the other person's body movement or speech pattern defeats the purpose of the technique. What you want to do is to make these movements flow naturally with what you are saying. Keep in mind that you are not a robot, and you definitely don't want the other person to catch on to what you are doing. So be mindful of how you shift your posture in response to theirs, how you tilt your head in response to theirs, and how you use your gestures in response to theirs. As with all things, moderation is important here.

You must not copy every single move the other person makes throughout your interaction.

Effective Listening
You cannot fake listening to someone when half of the time, your attention is clearly shifting from them to other things, like your

phone, computer, or other things happening around you. Conversely, you will overdo effective listening if you keep your attention riveted on the other person the entire time! What you should aim at is to show them that you are listening without appearing to be trying too hard.

Nodding is a sign that you are following what they are saying, and it nudges and encourages the other person to be more forthcoming. However, excessive nodding is a clear sign that you are not listening but simply want to appear that you are listening. It can also be a sign that you are trying to be a yes man or yes woman, agreeing "blindly" to whatever it is they are saying without thinking about it. This is usually a mistake that subordinates make with their bosses or employers. The other person will get a clear signal that you are not genuine in your agreement.

Use Their Name

This is one powerful "relaxation" trick salespeople use. When you use a person's name in a conversation, you are sending a powerful unconscious message to them to relax and trust you more. Even in writing (email, text messages, and so on), mentioning the other person's name helps to build rapport with them.

As an example, instead of saying, "I'd like you to consider the benefits of this proposal," you can create a stronger bond with the other person if you use their name like this: "Jane, I want you to consider how this proposal will benefit you." It doesn't matter if the other person is a complete stranger; using their name shows them you were interested in them right from the very first time they introduced themselves that you could remember their name.

Smile

A smile seems to appear simple; however, it is one of the most difficult to fake. The reason for this is simple: the muscles that move in your face during a genuine smile are controlled by impulses sent from the brain. You simply cannot fake those impulses. For this reason, I will strongly suggest that if you must fake a smile, do it from a distance so that the other person will not be able to clearly read your eyes (if they know how to detect a fake smile).

However, if you are in a close range and you must fake a smile, don't let the smile linger on your face. A brief smile will do the trick. Holding a fake smile on your face is a dead giveaway that you are not the real deal.

When you are in contact with someone and you want to relax a bit, flash a quick smile—not necessarily showing your teeth because that will make you look very awkward, especially if it is a fake smile. To add more effect, you can raise your eyebrows slightly to cover for the fake smile.

Faking Self-Confidence

There are several ways you can fake self-confidence using your body language. The thing with faking self-confidence is that the effect is not only felt on the people you are trying to manipulate or persuade; you eventually feel it too because, as I have earlier mentioned, your brain assumes that you are actually feeling that way and sends a rush of hormones to increase your self-confidence and decrease your stress level.

So, here are some quick body language tips to use in faking self-confidence.

Using Low Tone

Nervous and anxious people usually speak with high pitches and at a quicker pace, whether they are males or females. On the other hand, when you speak with a low tone and a slower pace (not a dull monotone voice!), it conveys a sense of authority or power.

Here is a simple trick you can use to lower the tone of your voice. Before you speak, tighten your lips together and make a humming sound for about ten seconds. This will return your voice tone to its optimal pitch. Also, when you finish your sentences, remember to make your voice drop at the end. This will make your voice sound more authoritative. When your voice goes high as you finish your sentences, it conveys a question rather than a statement or an order. It will sound like you are seeking approval from the other person or people listening to you.

Assume the Power Pose

When you need a quick boost of self-confidence, stand upright with your legs spread apart and your hands on your hips. Lift your head like someone who is truly confident and stay in that position for about two to three minutes. This is the power pose; it has the effect of increasing your self-confidence and making you calmer, especially when you are going into a meeting that makes you nervous.

Claiming Your Territory

When you sit, place your feet firmly on the floor, and you spread your arms on the table in front of you. You can even hang one hand behind the chair you are sitting on. This posture says you are in charge of your space. And even if you are not too sure of yourself inwardly, it doesn't show when you carry yourself in this manner. It is an excellent move to hide your inner fears.

NONVERBAL OF LEGS AND FEET

Like the other limbs, legs, and feet are used to communicate as a form of body language. If one is seated and continuously taps one of the legs on the floor, then the individual is not focusing on the conversation. The tapping of feet on the floor is a way for an individual to channel his or her energy elsewhere, and this denies the person the focus to process the body language of the speaker as well as the emotions. Different reasons can make one tap their feet on the floor, and one of them is an attempt to escape from a hurtful message. For instance, if the speaker is touching on a sensitive issue and is insensitive, then the part of the audience may continuously tap on the floor as a means of avoiding processing the message. Individuals with low concentration levels may inadvertently tap on the floor because they want a distraction.

Additionally, if one is speaking and stands on one leg, then the individual is feeling tense. When speaking before a large audience, one is likely to feel scared for a while before regaining confidence. In most cases, one will stand on one leg with the other leg folded at the knee-level and checked on the straight one akin to a flamingo standing. The posture serves a coping mechanism for the individual as he or she tries to process the stage fright without appearing visibly scared. In most cases, the individual will relax the folded leg and stand on both before reverting to this position. For most people, this body language usually is brief as the person quickly gains confidence and assumes normal body posture.

Similarly, standing with crossed legs at the ankle-level indicates that one is feeling unease with the speaker or the message. You probably have noticed that some people cross their legs in an alternating manner when speaking. If one crosses the legs when speaking, then probably the individual is feeling unease with the message or the audience. The crossing of the legs suggests that one is feeling defensive and wants to shield the personal space even further. In a manner, the individual is trying to safely process unwanted message or unwanted emotions by crossing the legs. For some reason, most shy people may cross their legs when speaking, which is an indication of being highly protective of their personal space.

If one sits on the chair and stretches both legs forward, then the person is feeling relaxed and casual. At home and especially when from work, you are likely to sit with all of your legs stretched straight forward as a way of relaxing. For this reason, this posture should be avoided in all formal settings such as workplaces. Chances are, if you were to visit someone with a managerial position and the person rocks the chair with both feet full stretched forward, then you will conclude that he or she is treating you casually. In most cases, this posture is realized when one is sitting on a raised or reclining chair.

Additionally, if one scratches the other leg using one of the legs, then the person is trying to get interested in the conversation. In most contexts, one will scratch one leg against the other as a way of eliminating a distraction such as an itch or recalling some information that will interfere with listening. For emphasis, if one scratches the other leg-using one of the legs, it does not necessarily mean that the individual is not listening. It is most likely a way of avoiding attending to the distraction, such as an itch or struggling with safely processing negative emotions such as anger. Most public speakers are likely to scratch one of their legs using the other when asked a disturbing question because this body language can be used as a coping mechanism for processing negative feedback.

Relatedly, sitting with both legs wide open, indicates disinterest in the conversation. Recall how you sit watching boring news or TV program. Most likely, you relax your legs far wide apart and in a slumped position when watching or listening to a dull interview or movie. For this reason, this posture should be avoided as it communicates tiredness and disinterest in the message as well as the speaker. Perhaps you noticed that during your high school days, some of your colleagues would exhibit this posture. Expectedly, men are likely to exhibit this posture due to cultural considerations that dissuade women from sitting in this posture.

If one sits upright with both knees nearly the same level and close enough, then the individual is highly alert and actively participating in the conversation. A person in this posture is fully occupying their personal space and feeling comfortable. Keeping the knees at the same level and close is a mechanism to enhance focus at the speaker or the message. During church sessions or a meeting of state officials, most members seated in a hall are likely to manifest this posture, and it is because they are deliberately trying to listen. Again, using the example of a school, chances are that during an address by the school principal, the students were neatly seated with their knees close to each other and the same level because they purposely wanted to remain alert.

BEHAVIORAL CUES

Correspondingly, stretching both legs straight while seated upright indicates the casualness of the person regarding the message or the speaker. As earlier on mentioned, if one sits with all the legs straightened and stretched, then the individual wants to induce relaxation and feel casual. At the end of a class, there are chances that you or one of your classmates stretched their legs while in a seated position to indicate that they are inducing relaxation and feeling casual than they were. While this posture appears like just any other posture, it can be important for an individual that is feeling restless. Using this posture, a restless individual can be helped to induce the much-needed relaxation of the body and mind.

Additionally, standing at the same spot for more than five minutes when speaking may indicate that one is not natural with the speaking. Indeed, standing at the same spot for more than five minutes indicates that one is operating under a fixed schedule and a defined set of expectations such as giving a speech or dictating notes to a class. For instance, a preacher is operating under fewer time constraints and expectations and will speak at random but predictable physical spots compared to a minister reporting on a disease outbreak. For this reason, the unrestricted movement of feet through walking indicates freedom of thought, unlike speaking at the same physical spot.

If one taps their feet on an object, then the person is not actively participating in the conversation. One of the best indicators that one is not listening to an interview is when the individual taps on the floor, desk, or wall. The tapping of feet on an object is an attempt to ease the mind of processing what is being said because it is demanding or disturbing. For instance, at one point, you noticed that one of your classmates taps on the wall or floor when talking about an essay or project because the colleague does not feel as good as others do. This behavior is meant to help the individual process negative feedback safely because continued active listening will make the individual get overwhelmed by emotions.

Furthermore, if one knocks against their knees, then the individual is feeling embarrassed or disinterested in the conversation. Knocking the kneecaps or shaking the legs with knees almost touching indicates uneasiness, inadequacy, and embarrassment. In most instances, this posture is attained when one is seated. Knocking of knees or almost knocking the knees against each other is also a way of expressing extreme anger where one tries to process the negative emotion safely. Either you or your colleagues probably waved their knees to almost touching because you were feeling frightened, intimidated, or upset and wanted to process the emotion safely. Since this posture is mostly done when one is seated, most speakers commonly miss it, but a keen observation of the shoulders may indicate the individual is waving the knees against each other.

Relatedly, if one places one or both of their palms in between their two thighs clamped together, then the individual is feeling embarrassed. Children commonly exhibit this posture, and it is meant to indicate that he or she is feeling cornered or embarrassed. Adults also manifest this posture of clamping one or both palms of the hands between their thighs when feeling embarrassed or scared. Fortunately, this posture can be observed with ease, and the message read accordingly. In some extreme circumstances, this posture communicates that one is feeling erotic or sexual, especially when done by one of the lovers towards the other.

If one walks excitedly across the stage when speaking, then the individual is likely to be excited. As earlier on suggested, moving animatedly across the stage or physical area where the communication is happening may suggest that one is happy and at ease with the message and the audience. Think of how preachers utilize the stage by moving animatedly across the stage. Most storytellers also utilize random and firm movements across the stage to indicate that they are feeling confident and involved in the message and the audience. Most artistes tend to move randomly and excitedly across the stage to show eagerness, happiness, and active participation of what they are delivering to the audience.

On the other hand, if one walks slowly across the stage when speaking, then the person is focusing more on the message content over everything else. When the speaker wants to draw attention to the message over everything else, then he or she will move slowly across the stage to ensure that the audience recalls more the words rather than the body language. For this reason, slowing down during speaking may help the audience lend more criticality to the message rather than the speaker antics. It is the reason why most interviews are conducted while one is seated. Even when given an entire stage, a politician is likely to move least because he or she wants the audience to remember the content of the message as opposed to other aspects of communication. In communication, any unwanted message is known as noise and if a speaker wants the audience to remember the presentation, and then, if the audience remembers the dressing or dancing of the speaker, then this can amount to noise. Noise in communication is thus contextual contrary to the broad assumption that noise in communication is always universal.

There is also the closed posture where one crosses the arms across the chest or crosses the legs away from someone or sits in a hunched forward position as well as showing the backs of the hands and clenching the fists are indicative of a closed posture. The closed posture gives the impression that one is bored, hostile, or detached. In this posture, one is acting cautious and appears ready to defend himself or herself against any accusation or threat. While we insist that certain postures should not be encouraged, it is important to realize that they should be expressed as they help communicate the true status of the individual.

For the confident posture, it helps communicate that one is not feeling anxious, nervous, or stressed. The confident posture is attained by pulling oneself to full height, holding the head high, and keeping the gaze at eye level. Then pull your shoulders back and keep the arms as well as the legs to relax by the sides. The posture is likely to be used by speakers in a formal context such as when making a presentation, during cross-examination, and project presentation. In this posture, one should stand straight and deliver the message.

Then there is the crossing of the legs from the thigh through the knee while seated on a chair, especially on a reclining chair. In this posture, one is communicating that he or she is feeling relaxed and less formal. In most cases, this posture is exhibited when one is at home watching a movie or in the office alone past working hours. If this posture is replicated in a formal context, then it suggests boredom or lack of concentration. If a speaker reads this body language, then he or she should realize that one of the members of the audience is feeling less interested in the message and should activate self-feedback. Self-feedback includes things such as am I speaking fast. Should I give them a break? Should I vary the tone?

For the posture where one crosses the legs from the ankle to the soles of the feet while seated, it communicates that one is trying to focus on an informal context such as at home. For instance, if a wife or a child asks the father about something that he has to think through, then the individual is likely to exhibit this posture. If this posture is replicated in a formal context, then it suggests boredom or lack of concentration. Akin to all aspects of communication, it is imperative that the audience generates feedback for the speaker to take into account and adjust accordingly. While some forms of body language indicate casualness, they are not entirely deliberate, and they are merely stating the true status of the affected individual. What is important is for the speaker to adjust the communication by simplifying it, introducing breaks, varying tone, and being sensitive about how the audience feels.

THE SECRET TO CHARISMA (OPENNESS)

Have you ever noticed that when you are around certain people, everything seems more upbeat and exciting? Do they seem full of confidence and happy to be there? Does the mood lighten, and it cheers you up to be in their company?

Then no doubt this person is charismatic. They are happy in their own bodies and with who they are. Because to make others feel good, you have to feel good about yourself and be able to exude an air of self-assurance as if you're not too unduly bothered about what others think of you. You are your own person and although you might respect their point of view, you also have your own opinions, which you consider valid. If you value yourself, then others are likely to as well. But how to you reach this heightened state?

Stand Tall
Your posture speaks volumes and, if you stand with your shoulders back and your back straight, looking slightly up, it will tell others that you are ready for anything and full of self-confidence. It's the exact opposite of slouching, which suggests someone is not feeling up to par and would rather not be seen in public. They're having a bad day. Standing straight or even sitting straight implies that you are relaxed and someone to be taken seriously.

When you walk into a room, there should be nothing tentative about your entrance. Stand proud and smile. Even if you are going into the room for business purposes, there is no reason why you shouldn't appear friendly. Be the first to put out your hand to shake theirs, confident it will be returned.

Make Someone Feel Special

We're all self-centered. We're only human and everyone enjoys it when the topic of conversation is themselves – despite insistence from them that it isn't the case. By showing that you're interested in someone else makes them warm to you.

But make that interest genuine. Everyone on earth has something interesting to offer, some story to their lives. Everyone thinks that they have a book within them and recently, with the advent of self-publishing, many get around to writing it and putting it out there. They think it will reap in millions and be a best-seller and they sit back and wait for the sales to rack up. They are then faced with huge disappointment because they don't sell any. None. Zero. Zilch. Who would be interested in a book about the life of someone they've never heard of? What makes their story more interesting than anyone else's? They want to hear about themselves, not you.

Then you come along and ask them questions about themselves and their life. Your interest is sincere, and they feel as if you are an empathic, intelligent and funny person. You've made them feel as if you're bonding because you're mirroring their body language and facial expression and they feel as if you are the first person in a long time that has come along and made an impression on them. Who could fail to respond favorably to someone who showed such genuine interest in them and really seemed to appreciate what they had to say?

But it is not just with that one person. It is with everyone you meet.

Shut Up and Listen

Too many of us prattle on, feeling that what we have to say is of great importance but the most important part of our body when bonding with others is our ears. If you let someone say their piece, they will never forget how much they enjoyed themselves in your company. They'll remember how lovely you were to talk to and how you laughed together. What a warm and generous person you are, and they will talk highly of you to others. Not only did you ask the questions, but you listened to the answers too and responded appropriately.

Time to Talk

Of course, there will be occasions that you must be the one doing the talking but there are things that can help you when you're on the other end of communication too. Have you every listened to a truly inspirational speaker and felt a cold shiver go down your back? Or been moved to tears or taking action? We don't have to look far to find someone: Martin Luther King, JFK, Churchill, Oprah, even Hitler moved millions to war.

But what do they have that the rest of us might not be using?

Getting the Results

Look the part. Dress to impress as if you care about your

appearance. If you want to make an impression, consider your audience and dress appropriately.

Know your stuff – Don't go into an interview or do a presentation without knowing your subject inside out. It's okay to be thrown by an odd question – or maybe even two – but to be constantly telling your audience that you'll get back to them just does not cut the mustard and you'll be regarded as an idiot.

Walk in there relaxed as if you have all the confidence you need to get through whatever ordeal is facing you. On the other hand, do not appear to be too cocky.

Have a sense of humor. Learn to laugh at yourself and be self-deprecating. No-one likes a showoff!

Look people in the eye and stand tall but relaxed.

Use gestures including some to involve your audience. You might stretch both arms out, with palms up indicating that you're all in this together.

Ask rhetorical questions and leave pauses giving them time to digest what you've said.

Be lively and interesting. Try not to stutter or hesitate. Speak out clearly and confidently and be enthusiastic about your subject. Make it clear that you love what you're doing.

Try and mention something that makes them identify with you, or that they can sympathize or empathize with.

Make them laugh. It doesn't have to be constant – unless you're a comedian doing it for a living. But inject some humor. Make them feel as if they've enjoyed themselves.

- Be inspirational. Make them go away uplifted, feeling as if everyone is wonderful, especially them. Make them believe that they can move mountains.

Anyone can learn the art of charisma. But it takes self-confidence and courage to sell snow to an Eskimo. You might be faking it to start with, putting on an act of bravado. Remember all the rules above and you'll soon be astonished how quickly they begin to take root and make you grow on the firm foundation of sincerity and liking other people. And most important of all: liking yourself.

Interviews And Power Plays

How do you get the job you've always dreamed of? Well, of course, there are some basics like have the relevant skills and qualifications. But what if you're one of six excellent candidates? How do you ensure that you stand out head and shoulders above the rest of them? What sort of things should you be aware of to make them remember you and make the rest sink into the background?

Well, rest assured, there are things that can make a difference and they are not all that hard for you to achieve. Let's get started.

Dress the Part

Remember to dress appropriately. You want to present a professional front not as if you're going to a club afterwards. Clothing should be smart and don't wear anything too tight or something you feel as if you have to constantly adjust or it will be considerably distracting. Don't forget the shoes. Nothing smacks of laziness more than unpolished, scuffed shoes. Remember hygiene. Do not wear too much perfume or cologne so that they interviewers are overpowered, and women should wear their makeup understated, not outlandish.

Make an Entrance

As soon as you set foot in the place, start as you mean to go on. If you have to wait in reception until the interviewers are ready to see you, be friendly with whoever is on reception. You don't know what office politics are like. It might even come down to the boss asking the receptionist what she thought. If you're friendly towards her, she'll remember you and say she liked you. Be confident and sit with an open body. Smile – but not too widely. Be natural. Make her laugh if you can.

Meeting the Interviewer

This can be a daunting experience and we can all remember when an interview went well and when they went bad. If you can't remember any in the latter category you're either very young or very lucky. Again, enter the room as if you mean business. Offer your hand for a handshake and make sure it's firm. If you feel as if your palm is sweating because of nerves make sure you wipe your hands inconspicuously before entering the room.

This should feel as if it has a two-way dynamic; after all, you want to know that you will be able to get on with your colleagues as well. Try and imagine that you are trying to get to know each other. As you would in any potential relationship, it's about sharing information and putting your best foot forward.

Posture

Sit straight up on the chair they offer and do not slouch under any circumstances. Sit straight on facing them. NEVER chew gum. If there is more than one interviewer try and make eye-contact with them all in turn and smile, exchanging pleasantries and thanking them for inviting you. Don't cross your legs but put both feet firmly on the floor.

If they give you a choice of straight back chair or comfy couch, choose the straight back. The last thing you want to do is sink suddenly into the couch and have your legs pointed in the air! And don't take them up on their offer of a hot drink. Water if you must but be careful not to spill it all over their shiny new desk.

Voice Pitch and Intonation

Do not allow your voice to become monotonous or drone on. If you think you are boring them, pick up your game a little and introduce something more exciting to recapture their interest. Perhaps you could inject a question to wake them up again. Speak clearly and at a measured pace. Do not speak too quickly or they will be exhausted trying to keep up with you.

No Fidgeting

If you have any nervous habits such as brushing back your hair with your hand, cracking your knuckles, sniffing or a nervous cough, make yourself aware of these and try your best not to send the interviewer around the bend.

Presentations

It's quite common now for companies to ask potential employees to do a presentation at their interview. This is your chance to make a lasting and deep impression upon them. A presentation is another word for gift and that's just what it is. If you're clever, you'll have included some visual aids, but not too many. Aids are there to help you – and the audience. They help you to keep you on track and they help the audience by clarifying points or breaking up sitting listening to you talk at them. Keep it sharp, witty and informative. And don't move around too much but there's nothing wrong with making gestures. At the end, ask for questions. And you should have the answers ready if you don't want to look foolish.

Any Questions

Any interviewer worth their salt will ask you this question. Be sure that you have some sensible and intelligent ones to hand. Don't ask things like, "What day do I get paid on?" A better question would be to ask where they see the company heading in the next five years. Turn it around so that they must do the talking and nod and offer the right reactions to let them know you're interested and on board.

Goodbye and Thank you

As you leave, shake each one of the interviewer's hands and thank them for seeing you, remembering to smile.

Leave the building.

And breathe.

Making a Good Impression

The most important impression that you can make is the first one and you will never get that chance again so make the most of it. The impression you want to leave them with is that you are the person for the job and that they hope that they'll be lucky enough to get you. How do you go about making that indelible impression on them?

If you think that they will like you on sight, they probably will.

Never forget to shake hands. If they don't offer theirs, offer yours anyway. They will notice.

Dress the part.

Be friendly. Smile.

Walk tall and straight.

Walk with a bounce in your step, not as if you've got rubber soles on but if you walk like this instead of gliding it tells people you're happy.

Smell nice but not overpowering.

Don't wear bright or garish lipstick.

Brush your teeth and be aware of personal hygiene.

- Never drink alcohol before an interview or the night before because sometimes it can be detected the day after.
- Make eye contact.
- Speak clearly and change your tone of voice.

- Mirror the interviewer's body language.
- Never chew gum.
- Don't slouch.
- Be interested in them.
- Don't be modest but don't be too cocky either.
- Know why you want the job.
- Have some (positive) things to say about your negatives such as I'm addicted to detail. Everything must be right.
- Be friend, but respectful.
- Use open body language.
- Don't cross your legs.
- Sit up straight.
- Sign on the dotted line!
- Thank them for offering you the job.

Detecting Lying And Deception

No-one likes a liar, but we all come across some very good ones along the way. And no doubt, we have all told some of our own whoppers or at least white lies in our time. We might do it to save someone's feelings, or because we're ashamed of what we've done or said. Sometimes, it can be blatantly obvious that someone is lying whilst others get away with murder without being caught.

And who can sincerely say that they appreciate sycophantic behavior in others? When we ask for a friend's opinion, we don't expect them to pay lip service or lie to us. What favor is it doing us if they allow us to go out in a hideous outfit just so that they won't have to tell us the truth and upset us? Ultimately, we are going to be a lot more upset when we see the spectacle we presented on Facebook when we had thought we looked fab.

Lying and deception runs along a spectrum and can range from a white lie to deceiving someone out of their life savings. Even trained investigators struggle with establishing what is true and what is not.

Some people make a living out of it, selling products that do not exist. This becomes even easier when it is done over the telephone and you have no other cues than what you are hearing. For instance, a couple was desperate for a loan and they see an ad online which promises that their loan application will be more or less guaranteed. They call the company and a nice, smooth-talking young man takes their details, including their bank details. They pay a deposit for administration costs, which the nice young man says will not be refundable. He even asks them that they agree to that but reassures them that he is almost positive that they will be approved for the loan. Of course, there is no loan but the couple that are desperate for the loan are even more desperate now having paid a hefty 'deposit'. All it takes to earn a lot of money doing this is an absence of morals and conscience and a lot of desperate trusting people.

It could be as innocuous as, "Yes, this stew is fabulous," when your partner is proud of the dish she's spent hours making. Even though you might be thinking to yourself, "I hope she never makes this again though, so I had better not be too enthusiastic."

Perhaps, though, you find a receipt for an overnight stay in your partner's pocket. How do you think you would tackle that? Do you think if you addressed the problem that you could spot the tell-tale signs that they might be lying?

How can we tell if someone is lying to us?

Are they touching their noses? Or trying to cover their mouths? They might to hide the fact that they are lying and be nervous about giving anything away so that their hand is drawn to their face to obliterate signs of lying.

Are they looking you straight in the eyes or looking down, unable to meet your eyes. Hopefully, that's because they are feeling shame at being insincere. Sometimes, when people are lying they look to the left because they are trying to conjure up the image they are projecting and trying to think of credible answers to your questions. If their eyes go to the right, they are trying to remember things that they have heard or seen. Don't confuse a lack of eye contact with a lack of confidence though. Quite often, people who have low self-esteem find it difficult to look someone in the eye. Normally, it's around 50% of the conversation. Conversely, if someone makes a point of looking you straight in the eyes for the whole conversation, it might feel unnatural because it is. It's what's known as the bare-faced lie.

Does the tone of their voice change? Quite often, when people lie a subtle change in tone can be detected. On the other hand, the change could be quite marked to indicate that they perceive an accusation as audacious. Or it may be that the language they use is different too. If a lie is pre-determined they might have thought up elaborate details, which someone who is telling the truth would not so readily divulge at such length. Are they stammering? Or do you notice that they cough to clear their throat, giving them time to think up the next lie?

Does their body go rigid? When someone is relaxed, they tend to be more fluid in their movements, perhaps using their hands for expression. When they are lying, they try and control clues, which might escape to give the game away and so hold themselves tightly in check.

Is there a mismatch between what they are saying and what they are thinking? This might be congratulating someone on a promotion, but their tone of voice is anything but congratulatory. Instead, their face might exhibit contempt because they are thinking that the promotion is undeserved. Don't turn your back on this person!

Are there a lot of pauses between answers or sentences? This could mean that the person is putting a lot of thought into what they are saying or that they are taking their time to thinking up believable stories.

Are they adding a lot of details to their account? Have you ever heard someone say that they made up such a good story that they believed it themselves? This could almost be true. The liar is so convinced that their story is realistic they are also convinced that the person they are telling it to must believe it too.

- Are they becoming defensive and trying to shift the blame? Does their tone rise? Are they blushing? Are they going pale?

This is not an exhaustive list, but the point is that you should combine as many signals together as possible. If a person you know is acting out of character, then it is highly likely that something is amiss. Investigate it further. Ask questions and watch carefully for reactions.

UNDERSTANDING CUES - CONTEXT IS KING

So, having looked at what body language is in a base sense, it's now time to study and identify some of the main components that comprise of this non-verbal framework. This is a reasonably important step in the process in order to give you some context about a situation before critically assessing the meaning behind any specific body language movement or gesture. You need to ensure you are interpreting things through the correct lens.

However, the rules aren't hard and fast here. Is a person clenching their hands and folding their arms because they feel threatened? Or are they feeling discontented or perhaps just cold? The answer to this will depend on a variance of factors which you will need to successfully appraise beforehand. So, here are the five main contextual factors to pay attention to, to hopefully help you do just that.

Cues

Essentially when humans act, it's very seldom done in isolation. We do things in response to others doing things as part of a sequence or "loop" of behaviors which feed into one another. A cue simply refers to the initial action or stimuli produced by the environment or other person which will intern elicit or "trigger" a certain response from within us.

If you observe a particular body movement or gesture from another person, this will be the initial cue to start interpreting why they are showing us what they are. These gestures will also start to give away what they may be thinking or feeling to produce that expression or posture in the first place.

These cues will almost always be subconscious emotional reactions to either the outside stimulus or the internal feeling concerning it. As we have seen already with regards to the limbic system, these reactions will be instinctive and difficult to suppress. If a person has just been given some bad news they maybe hunched over with their head down. The action will usually inadvertently give away the cue by its very nature. You can reverse engineer their thought process in the vast majority of cases.

Changes

This might be from a predominantly open stance to a more closed and defensive posture. From a standing position with arms by the side to retreating to a seated position with arms and/or legs crossed.

Something will have initiated this change and it's your job to identify the cue responsible for it. Does the person now feel more threatened? Or perhaps they are trying to conceal something? Are they now looking away, which might indicate that they are being dishonest or even lying to you?

This may work both ways, I.e. in a positive or negative sense. Salespeople will watch for these changes which can often just be subtle gestures to indicate if a person is either warming up to what they are saying, and therefore it's time to move onto the next stage of closing. Or a regression in body language to signal a step back in the process, and a need to further qualify the customer and get them back onside.

I picked up on these things very quickly in my early business career as I was fortunate enough to have a mentor who would point them out for me. Regardless of what they might be, these transitions can be very significant and therefore very important to pick up on.

Clusters

Similar to the concept of behaviors occurring within a sequence, body language transitions and changes rarely happen in isolation, but rather in clusters. When analyzed more closely they will happen in groups of movements as opposed to a standalone gesture which usually ensures they are easier to identify.

Humans are pattern seekers by very nature so this should come somewhat naturally to everyone. But really honing in on these clusters of gestures can really give you a better idea of what the other person is feeling and thinking.

That being said, there are instances where a simple flicker of an eye lid is all you have to go off. However, in most cases people will typically go through a range of movements which are far easier to spot, and tend to provide a much more reliable indicator when translating these movements into the potential feelings and meaning behind them.

For instance, returning to the example above, a person may go from initially standing with their hands in a neutral position to sitting down, leaning back, arms folded with a frowning facial expression. Something has now obviously changed, and the sequence or "cluster" of movements will be enough to clearly indicate this.

In reality, when a person does this, they are often times attempting to subconsciously signal what they are thinking. They aren't trying to be deceitful here. Whether it's consciously done or not, these overt changes in movement are usually intentional displays of a person's displeasure or joy, if done in the reverse. As I mentioned previously, a lot of our natural body language was the only means of communicating before modern day speech, so the idea wasn't to hide it at all.

However not all these cluster movements are so easy to follow. They can be mixed signals and contradictory in nature. A scratching of the head or neck combined with a smile seemingly say's two different things. 1) That the person is potentially being deceitful and attempting to conceal something 2) Additionally portraying an open sign of endearment and affection.

Or is the smile a nervous one which in fact vindicates the first assumption? This is where your analyzing skills and experience will come into play.

Character/Culture

Another factor to take into consideration when assessing the behavior and body language of others is the overall character of the person in question. But also the culture in which they were raised in. This will obviously be greatly dependent on how well you know the individual, and how familiar you are with their conversing and interaction habits.

Is the person more extroverted by nature and likely to display larger and more overt gestures naturally? If this is the case then some of their gestures and movements can be discounted and considered less significance, as this is their baseline behavior. I had a specific college friend who would literally never stop talking. She would almost shout every sentence in addition to this. This was simply her default demeanor.

Conversely, the introverted individuals among us usually express more subtle and concise body language gestures and shouldn't be analyzed as being unhappy necessarily, but rather just a consequence of their default behavior.

You can obviously still watch out for the changes in these people as something done out of character can be a clear giveaway to a change in feeling and emotion. This is likely due to a result of some environmental or internal cue. So try to analyze the people you are observing through the lens of their individual personality traits, and adjust your thinking accordingly.

A similar consideration should be made regarding the individual's background and culture. I have had the opportunity to travel to almost every continent, and I can assure you that whilst the base needs of humans remain the same (as Maslow's Pyramid shows us) the way in which people express themselves can certainly differ.

If a western person were to walk down a busy market street in Dubai, Doha or Damascus, they would be forgiven for thinking that everybody was full scale arguing with one another. Like my college friend who used a similar interaction style in her conversations! It would seem hostile, when in fact this is the default way most Middle Eastern populations converse.

On the other hand, if you were to sit a business meeting in Asia, especially Japan or Singapore, you would be forgiven for thinking that everyone in the room is being dismissive or potentially even rude. However this is in fact their default conversational style, and is much more indirect in nature.

The final consideration is that of somebody's age and gender relative to the body language behavior they are likely to display. More pronounced and energetic gestures made by teenage males can somewhat be discounted as business as usual. As once more, it's their default behavior for the most part. Likewise, more conservative and less pronounced gestures and modest postures of elderly women will serve as their baseline reading, as opposed to an inherent assumption of unease or distress.

In general I would say women actually have a better overall perception and ability to analyze others compared to their male counterparts. This is thought to be at least in part due to the evolutionary need to more reliably assess potentially threatening behavior from others, especially larger males, in order to protect their offspring. This may not be the case so much today, however women definitely still retain this ability to interpret body language signals to great effect.

In addition to having a greater innate ability to read others, females also have a higher propensity for more empathetic behaviors which was once again an evolutionary legacy in order to attract & retain partners and offspring. Empathetic personality types in general will be able to more accurately pick up on body language subtleties, so you are at an advantage if this is you.

Of course shorter term situational factors, such as mood and temperament will also play a part in someone's actions within all of the scenarios described previously, so this is not a cut and dry strategy by any stretch of the imagination. But it is certainly wise to take all of these variables into consideration when assessing a persons potential intentions behind their behavior, so you can better analyze them as a result.

Context

Finally, there is one other variable to take into consideration when assessing the behavior and body language of others, and that is the broader context to which the current situation is occurring. Similar to judging the character of others when it comes to analyzing others, we will all interpret these factors based on our own personal contexts.

However in general you need to assess exactly what is happening within the environment you find yourself in. If you are in more of a business setting, people's postures and gestures are naturally more likely to be upright and serious. Conversely, they will naturally be more open and loose within relaxed social settings.

This may seem like stating the obvious. But often these wider contextual factors will give away the underlying reason for a person's current body language. So do not discount them in the slightest.

The five factors I have explained within this chapter should be considered as overarching principles more than anything. Variables to take into consideration when assessing the body language and analyzing others. They are a compass and preparation step to set the tone and provide guidance for the specific and individual scenarios, which you will find yourself in within everyday situations.

You have to take these factors into account and modify your filters for assessment accordingly. That's not to say you should lean too heavily on them or become closed minded to new information about a situation. They are a crutch for analysis and nothing more. However do ensure you read over these principles once more to give yourself the proper grounding before moving onto the more practical steps which follow.

MEETING SOMEBODY

First impressions are some of the most important parts of meeting something or starting a relationship. A person makes their first impression quickly when they meet somebody. A person has made their first impression within the first 30 seconds of a conversation. The wrong types of body language can end up creating a false impression because people pay attention to the nonverbal language before listening to what you say.

When you learn how to interpret body language, it will help you to not only read people but it will improve your first impressions as well. First impressions depend completely on the nonverbal cues. Positive impressions typically involve:

- Keeping appropriate eye contact.
- Not searching the room with your eyes.
- Focusing on the other person.
- Eye contact should not feel like a stare down.
- Standing straight with your chest centered and shoulders back.
- Pay attention to what the conversation is focused on.

People who are looking to establish a good relationship will make sure that they keep an open posture. They will make sure to show the inside of their palms regularly, which lets the other person know that they are welcomed and what they are saying is important.

The trick about this is if you want to make a good impression, you also have to feel it on the inside. If you plan on showing complete integrity on the outside, you must make sure you feel it on the inside.

We're going to walk through the small little things that you should look for when a first meet a person. The slight movements, body position, and gestures of a person can let you know whether they really what to be talking to you, and so much more. You can also use this information to make sure that you make a good first impression.

Handshake

Think back to grade school when you were taught how to shake hands "correctly." You were supposed to have a firm, hard grip. Nobody likes to be handed a fish when shaking hands. It doesn't matter if you're an important person or well-educated, those few seconds it takes to shake hands can tell the other person more about you than any college degree ever could.

All over the world, a handshake is a way to say hello. While it can look like a simple friendly gesture, it can also cue you in on their personality. Therefore it is important to understand the meanings of handshakes in certain situations.

Handshakes start a conversation in almost any type of gathering. This can end up making or breaking the feel of the environment. There was a study published in the Journal of Personality and Social Psychology that explained that people should pay attention to how a person shakes hands. People make judgments and opinions based on this.

During 2000, the University of Alabama conducted a research study where they studied the handshakes of 112 people and compared the impressions they created with the paperwork they had to fill out.

It was discovered that a firm handshake was connected to traits like extroversion and being open to things. Weak handshakes were most connected to higher levels of shyness and anxiety. The women tended to have weaker handshakes than the men did, but women who did have a firm handshake were positively rated. No matter what sex a person is, strong handshakes equaled a strong personality.

The factors they used to judge the handshakes were complex. The people asked to judge underwent a month of training and were taught to look out for eight things:

Temperature

Completeness of grip

Dryness

Duration

Texture

Strength

Vigor

Eye contact

That's a lot to think about when all you want to do is shake their hand and figure out what their personality is like. The easy thing about this was that all the characteristics related to one another, and all it boiled down to people looking at firm, weak, positive impression, and weak impression. Those who maintained eye contact, held firm, shook with vigor and had warm strong hands were seen with positivity. That means that if a person has a firm handshake, then they have all the other characteristics.

Body Orientation

I want to take you on a bit of visualization. Imagine this, you are at the grocery store and you see a person you went to high school with at the other end of the aisle and you decide to say help. You turn and walk back to him. Yes, you have your back turned towards him, just hang on for a second, there is a point.

When you get closer to him, judging by the shadow that you see on the floor, you say, "Hi Steven. What have you been up to?" This is going to freak him out when he turns around, but it shows how important body orientation is. You could stand there and continue to talk to him with your back to him, but it would be pretty much impossible to hold a conversation.

There is an unwritten rule of keeping the correct body position when you have a conversation with a person. The body will naturally turn to the things you want.

You are likely thinking, "I already knew that. So what? If I need to get something out of the cabinet, I face the cabinet. You face the TV when you watch television." It's no big deal, right? This is an example where an important piece of information gets taken for granted.

During a conversation, we will turn towards the person we want to engage with. The way we keep our body oriented shows a lot about the things we are interested in. When two people are talking, you can figure out how involved they are by looking to see if they are parallel.

When two people are talking, they face each other and keep their shoulders parallel to each other. This creates a closed formation. This position means that they are physically and psychologically rejecting all the other people around them to focus on each other. This is probably something you have intuitively spotted before but think about this in a group setting where there are more than two people.

When there is a group of people talking, you can spot the people who are more interested in each other by looking for people who are standing parallel. If you see a conversation between three people, and two of them are standing parallel, then it would be easy to assume that they are trying to push out the third person, or the third has partially removed their self from the conversation.

There may be a chance that the third person wants to join the conversation, but it a part of a different group. If you try to draw a straight line from one person in the direction they are pointed, you are going to reach another person that they are interested in and want to engage with.

Now, when that third person tries to join in a conversation with two people who are visibly parallel, there are two things that could happen. That person is either going to be rejected or welcomed.

How can you figure out what is going to happen by watching their body language?

Welcomed

If the third person is welcomed into the conversation, the other two will need to change their position to allow them in. They are starting in a parallel position, focused on each other, but as the third person comes in, they will both have to give a bit of attention to him. They have to switch up their orientation to redistribute their attention.

They should both pivot so that they are standing at a 45-degree angle to each other so that they form a triangle. This gives everybody in the group equal attention. If there are two people talking and standing at a 45-degree angle, it could mean that they are looking for another person to join their conversation, or they aren't that interested in each other. They will gladly let a third person join their conversation.

Rejected

What if they don't want that third person in their conversation? When the third person approaches them, they will look over at him to reply to whatever he may have said, but they don't open up their body orientation to let him in. They are trying to reject him, at least at this moment.

It doesn't mean that they hate him; they simply don't want somebody interrupting their conversation. They are nonverbally letting him know, "We are in a private conversation, please leave us alone." For the most part, the person will take the hint and walk away. If they are desperate, though, the third person may try to force his way in.

This can be spotted in several group settings, and it doesn't just include groups of three. The more people you have talking to each other, the more circular the group will turn so that all their attention is distributed. If people don't have their attention equally distributed, there are likely some outcasts in the group.

Now, there are a few caveats you have to on the lookout for. If you spot people who are talking that aren't parallel to one another, that don't mean that they aren't interested in each other. If they are walking or done something that requires them to move, having this non-parallel position doesn't always show non-involvement.

People are also viewed as aggressive if they walk right up to another person, so this is the reason why most of us will approach people at a 45-degree angle so that we come off as more positive and there is a better chance of being accepted into the conversation.

In order to know whether two people in a non-parallel conversation aren't interested in one another, there are other things that you have to look at. For example, if they are looking around the room and aren't talking much, then there is a good chance they aren't into each other.

RAPPORT IN PRACTICE—USE UNCONSCIOUS COMMUNICATION CONSCIOUSLY

Take a deep breath. From this chapter and from the following, you will receive so much information in the form of facts, methods, and techniques of establishing rapport. You will learn everything that you may need, from body language to life views. Of course, you will have to put all this into practice, and the sooner you start, the better. But only without haste: do the exercise in the rhythm in which you are comfortable.

Do not be afraid to be "caught in the act" when trying to establish rapport. I assure you that no one will object to communicate with a pleasant and amiable companion who thinks the same way.

Move The Body! How To Use Body Language

I have already said that we create rapport, adapting to the interlocutor. We do this in several ways. First, mirroring the movement of the interlocutor, that is, using body language. I myself do not like the expression "body language". The word "language" evokes associations with what can be learned from textbooks and dictionaries. Of course, there are textbooks of body language. In them, you can read that the little finger set aside means this, and tapping with your left foot — this. Unfortunately, things are not as simple as they seem. Our gestures mean different things in different situations. For example, you probably heard that folded hands on the chest mean "doubt/disbelief," but this completely ignores the context in which a person performs this action.

You yourself probably thought that the interlocutor, crossing his arms over his chest, thus demonstrates how angry he is. But it was possible that at that moment he was cold and he crossed his arms to warm himself. Or it was just easier for him to stand with arms folded across his chest. To find out the true thoughts of a person, not enough crossed hands, you need to look for other signals. Is he tense or relaxed? What is his facial expression? Is it cold or warm in the room? Did you argue up to this point or peacefully talked?

That is why I do not like the phrase "body language". I would replace it with another concept, such as "body communication," although it sounds a bit awkward. But I will not overload the already overused dictionary of psychologists and use the fact that there is. Just let us agree: the term "body language" implies much more than just crossed arms or a pinky set aside.

Mirroring and Joining

How to use body language to establish rapport? Everything is very simple: you need to repeat, you must become the echo of your interlocutor. How? Carefully observe the interlocutor: how he holds his back, how his hands are folded, etc., and do the same. If a person moves with one hand, you repeat the movement. This can be done in two ways, which are called joining (match, from English. Match—matching) and mirroring. Often, both methods are called attachment, since they have the same effect. You can choose the method depending on the behavior of the interlocutor. If the interlocutor moves his right hand, you also move the right hand— this is a connection, it is convenient to use it when you are in close proximity to your interlocutor, for example, sitting next to him. When mirroring, you react with the opposite side of your body: it moves with your right hand, with your left hand, like a reflection in a mirror. Mirroring is good to use when you are standing or sitting against each other.

Your reaction must be very subtle. If you repeat the movements of the interlocutor too explicitly, he will naturally find such an abrupt change in contrast to your usual behavior strange and unnatural. If you suddenly begin to copy the movements of the interlocutor, then you will not be able to install rapport, because a person will have doubts about your mental state. It is necessary to adapt to the interlocutor carefully and imperceptibly. Move in small steps. Determine the rhythm, relying on the reaction of the interlocutor. If he looks interested and relaxed, you can safely resort to the technique of joining or mirroring.

At the beginning of communication, you can use the so-called representative system. This means that you repeat the movement of the interlocutor to a small extent (that is, coding, masking them). This way, the other person will not notice that you are trying to adapt to him (her).

Another way to mask your actions is to slow them down (for example, to pause before repeating the interlocutor's action). Subconscious counterparts will register your actions and interpret them correctly, while he himself will not notice your attempt to establish rapport. You can also copy the expression of the interlocutor. A man, after all, cannot see what he looks like at the moment of conversation with you. However, his face often reflects thoughts and emotions (body and mind are interrelated—do not forget about it). Seeing your expression, he realizes that you feel the same as he does. Since we do not see our face, we will not be able to notice that someone copies his expression. It is only necessary to make sure that the person's facial expression is accurately interpreted. Some people look angry or sad at the moment when they are just relaxed. Only then will everything look natural.

Try to adjust to the rhythm of the movements of your interlocutor. Your movements should be interactive, like during a handshake: a slow-moving person is shaken slowly, and vice versa. Other movements (for example, a nod of the head) should also be performed in the rhythm characteristic of the other person.

Do Not Think Too Much

As I already wrote, our actions are not uniquely interpreted by different people, but still, each person is inclined to use the same gestures in similar situations. Do not try to interpret the gestures of another person at the first meeting, instead just watch. Mark the movements, but do not rush to conclusions: this does not mean that your interlocutor is nervous. After some time you will learn to associate a certain movement with the state of a person. Having mastered the body language of your interlocutor, you will soon notice that you began to guess his next word. Here is the reading and analyzing of thoughts. You can begin!

Watching other people, you will notice what they themselves do not notice—changes in their body language. For example, when we are afraid, our face pales. When we are confused, we blush, but the face does not always blush, sometimes only the ears or the forehead blush.

Body Language As Medicine

As I said, one of the goals of establishing rapport is the ability to force a person to do what you want, or rather, to bring him to it. Rapport creates all conditions for the fulfillment of your desires, unless, of course, there will be a disconnection. Remember: changing the interlocutor's body language, you change his attitude towards you. Body and mind are interrelated—what happens in the body is interpreted in the head.

This circumstance can be used to improve relationships with friends and relatives. You can easily do it yourself. For example, you have a friend who often suffers from bouts of melancholy without particularly compelling reasons (for example, the salary was delayed or the day was overcast). Try to repeat the language of his body, but more hidden (restrained) movements. It is necessary to install rapport and make a friend understand that you are with him, that you know what he is like. When rapport is established, begin to change the signs of body language to more open, more positive ones, and do it gradually. Straighten your back, move your arms, smile. You will see, your friend will soon begin to repeat after you. Feel that the contact is lost—go back a step and start again. Move carefully: two steps forward, one step back.

Changing the body language of a sad person, you changed his mood. There is no trace of melancholy. It is difficult to go with a straight back and smile while maintaining a bad mood. Try it yourself and see for yourself!

However, remember, this technique does not help if a person has really severe depression. Then he just needs to cry. Suffering is a state of the body that allows you to save energy, while our brain thinks over the situation and is looking for a way out. If you try to establish rapport with a person in a state of deep depression, you can stop him from handling the situation that is necessary to get out of depression. Rapport will help only with mild sadness.

At first, it may seem to you that you are doing something unnatural, that it is not you, but someone else who is trying to establish rapport. But remember how you learned to ride a bike. At first, it was difficult, but soon you were already boldly pedaling, not understanding how this simplest occupation could so difficult. This is how the fourth stage is reached when cycling has become an unconscious knowledge, a part of the person himself, as he becomes a part of the technique of creating rapport. You just need to start.

How Do You Use Your Voice?

An important rapport creation tool is your own voice. The secret is the same: you imitate the interlocutor's intonations and the rhythm of his speech. Of course, this should be done carefully (not so clearly) and gradually, as with signs of body language, and it is not necessary to create a one-hundred-percent copy, because your companion will seem strange if you suddenly speak to a tee like him. Moreover, it is very difficult to imitate someone else's voice, which is why there are so few people capable of imitating the speech of famous people. But you can always find one feature that you can imitate.

Tone

Is the voice low or high? Men often have a low voice, and women have a high voice, and this is influenced by the culture of the society in which we live. It seems to women that they should speak in a feminine way, that is, in a high and clear voice, while men are trying with all their might to make their voices low and coarse. As a result, we often speak with undue effort, indistinct and inexpressive.

Depth

Interesting fact: we believe that a deep, low voice belongs to a serious person who can be trusted, while a high voice is associated with female frivolity or childishness.

Melody

A monotonous voice does not change in the course of a speech, even in interrogative or exclamatory sentences. Therefore, it is often difficult to understand what a person with such a voice really means: is he joking or speaking seriously? Asks or approves? Opposite to him is considered a melodious voice, rich in iridescent, melodious and expressive.

Pace

Does the person speak quickly or slowly? We speak at the same pace in which we think, and if you speak too slowly, your interlocutor gets tired and starts thinking about something else. In the worst case, he can't wait until you are finally done. If you speak too quickly, there is a risk that your partner will not have time to catch all the important points.

Strength Volume

I recommend choosing this particular role to follow. The one who speaks softly and gently will appreciate if you will do the same (this also applies to a loud, resonant voice). By the way, if you want your interlocutor to speak more quietly, you need to try to speak even louder—and he will immediately pay attention to the timbre of his voice (usually people do not notice this).

As you can see, there are many characteristics in the voice that can be repeated. The best thing is probably to start at a pace: rapport depends largely on the synchronization of movements—and the pace can stimulate a good result. Some argue that the pace of speech is a crucial tool in establishing rapport. I do not know if they are right or not, but the voice, for example, is very important when talking on the phone, because then it is our only tool for establishing contact with the interlocutor.

In the United States, one study was conducted, ordered by a company that sold goods over the telephone. They sold a newspaper subscription and wanted to increase the number of customers. For the experiment, the employees were divided into two groups: one continued to work, as before, the other received orders to speak at the same pace as the person on the other end of the line. With only this difference in the technology of negotiations, the second group increased the number of sales by 30 percent. The first group sold the same amount as before the experiment. Agree, 30 percent is not bad at all, especially when this indicator depends on whether you speak slowly or quickly.

Exercise On The Movement

1. When you next visit a restaurant, pay attention to the people between whom rapport is established. Choose a couple of lovers or a couple of old friends and see how they talk to each other in turn, how they copy their body language, how they understand each other perfectly.

2. Pay attention to their postures: most likely, they will even sit in the same way.

3. On the bus, tram or subway car, try to guess who are traveling together. Hint: they will sit the same and move the same. You always figure out a loving couple or friends, even if they were not able to sit next to each other in a crowded bus.

Exercises for the Shy

If you still feel shy to repeat the interlocutor's movements, try the following exercises.

1. Watch talk shows on TV. Take the same pose as the speaker and repeat his movements. Soon you will notice that you are guessing what this person will say in the next moment. There is nothing strange in this: movements express our thoughts. Repeating movement after someone, you start the same mental processes in yourself and start to think and feel like him.

2. Try to set rapport at a distance. While in a public place, select a person at the other end of the room and begin to repeat his or her body language. After a couple of minutes, he (or she) could easily come up to you and ask: "We are not familiar with each other?" But how else? After all, you are a mirror image of this person. Therefore, it is better to choose someone with whom you would be pleased to communicate, and not some nasty type. This method can be used to get acquainted with a beautiful girl (a handsome young man).

3. You can get rid of the fear of "being caught at the scene of a crime" by letting the other person talk about themselves. While he speaks enthusiastically about himself, you openly copy the signs of his body language, occasionally repeating "yup" and "uh", showing interest. When we talk about ourselves (and also when we are very angry), we abstract away from the outside world. At such a moment we are talking about ourselves and for ourselves, not noticing anyone or anything around.

What Gives Us Away?

Our Expressions

It will be a question of directly relating to verbal communication, but once again, I want to draw your attention to this. We all use the language differently: everyone has their own favorite words and expressions, the list of which I quote below. Here they can be copied, and it is quite plausible.

Slang

Slang words and expressions are difficult to copy because their use is determined by geographic, age and fashion trends. Slang is changing every day, and the fact that it sounded so "cool" yesterday, today is sent "to crap." If you are free to navigate the expressions your interlocutor uses, then feel free to copy it. But if you have no idea what "shoelaces" means, then it is better not to: you can go crazy. Slang also symbolizes belonging to a certain group (for example, age group), and in some cases, only those who are admitted to the group can use slang words, so you risk causing the anger of the interlocutor.

Professional Slang

Often, in a conversation on a particular topic, we need special words and terms. Each area has its own professional jargon. These special words will help you gain the confidence of the interlocutor. It is only important not to overdo it: use just as much jargon as the counterpart does in conversation. If you understand computers perfectly and your interlocutor pokes a finger at the screen with the words: "This thing doesn't work," you shouldn't go into the technical details, just ask if he tried to press the green button.

Personal Features

Although we spend much of our life at school and at the university, few of us speak the way it is recommended in language textbooks. We all just adore the words-parasites. No matter how awful they sound, if your interlocutor uses them, then you will have to.

Remember, we speak at the same speed as we think. If you speak slowly, your interlocutor is bored with you. Speak too fast—he does not have time to follow the course of your thoughts. Therefore, you need to speak at one pace, convenient for you and your interlocutor.

Favorite words

We all have favorite buzzwords. We use them often and in a variety of situations. These can be slang words, jargon and even swear words. We usually adopt them from other people. Sometimes we ourselves do not like such frequent use, and, once again catching ourselves on the word "drop dead", we exclaim: "We must finally get rid of this terrible expression!" But there are other, less noticeable words. Milton H. Erickson, one of the gurus of modern hypnotherapy, calls them "trans words." No, this is not related to transvestites, but to a hypnotic trance. You can very quickly install rapport, repeating trans words of a person. Speaking in his language, you show that you are set up just like him, and therefore you understand him.

It seems to you, I demand from you the impossible? Is it possible at the same time to imitate the voice, look for special words and repeat them and at the same time not forget what you, in fact, were going to say? Believe me, this is not as difficult as it seems. I have already said that unconsciously you repeat the body language of the interlocutor, the same with voice and manner of speaking. You are already doing this, which can be demonstrated. Remember the following situation. You end up talking on a cell phone, hang up, and everyone in the room knows who you just talked to (and you didn't call your interlocutor by name). Nevertheless, they guessed it. Do you recognize the situation? They understood who you communicated with because you spoke like him that is, adjusted to his manner of speaking. Most likely it was an old friend with whom you have rapport. We all want to be accepted and respected. We are all looking for social communication. We all want to create rapport.

Breathe, Patience, Breathe

One of the main rules for establishing rapport is proper breathing. However, most non-verbal communication specialists forget to tell you how difficult it really is to adapt to the breath of another person—a breath that we do not see. This requires a lot of training, but it is possible, and it needs to be done.

Observe how a person breathes, deeply or superficially, with his chest or diaphragm—this is visible in his stomach, chest, shoulders, and neck. Listen to the interlocutor's speech: in the pauses in a conversation, you can understand how often he breathes in the air.

Why do I need to imitate the interlocutor's breath? To adapt to the rhythms of his body. Changing the rhythm of breathing, you automatically change the rhythm of speech and body movements, and this helps to establish rapport.

I have already said that you need to adapt to the body language of your partner so that the rapport between you is not interrupted. Before you copy your partner's breath, feel his rhythm, try to just breathe in that rhythm, and not repeat every breath of your interlocutor. The most important thing is synchronization at a basic level, the rest will come later.

By breathing, you can also determine the mood of a person. This may be necessary for a situation where rapport is installed, but you feel that something is wrong with the other person. Listen to his breath. If he breathes intermittently and quickly, although outwardly he seems calm, it means he does not want to give out his excitement. This can say a lot. Different emotions are associated with different types of breathing.

Cozy Exercise

If you have a person, you can hug at any time (for example, a wife/husband), then hug him tightly and listen to his breathing. Breathe to the beat. Change the rhythm. If your partner unknowingly changed the rhythm of breathing, it means that you managed to establish rapport.

Martin Nyurap and Ian Harling in their book Equilibrium offer to try it without clothes. If you are so lucky that you have someone hugging without clothes, try to synchronize the breath. Now, on the contrary, breathe faster or slower than your partner. You will notice transitions in their mood—from a sense of community and almost to dislike—despite the fact that you, naked, hug each other.

Think About Energy

Imagine that you see your interlocutor from a short distance, the whole thing. Using this technique, one can determine the energy level of a person by his posture, breathing, and other factors. Some people are more passive in the first half of the day—their activity is awakened after dinner. In the morning they come to work, mumble "good-naturedly" and flop down on a chair, showing with their whole appearance that they should be left alone at least until 11–12. And only after lunch and the fifth cup of coffee, they get out of their shells and begin to communicate with others. This does not mean that they do not work well, no, this only means that they need to warm up properly before actively contacting other people. Sometimes even five cups of coffee help. These are typical representatives of the "Oysters", and for them, it is a completely natural state.

Then there is another type of people—the exact opposite of Oysters. These people are always full of energy, like Duracell batteries. They run in the mornings, come to work half an hour before everyone else, smile widely, and at lunch run to play a game of squash.

I once worked with a colleague who had six children. He came, or rather, came to work on a bicycle half an hour before everyone else, and all this time he was engaged in recording video of children on DVDs, which he took over the weekend, printed out covers and signed to see where the movie was. He is not an Oyster, he is a typical Rabbit from a Duracell battery advertisement.

Maybe you are one of those who come to work full of energy and the desire to create and find there sleepy, tired colleagues whose help is simply necessary, then you must reduce your activity. Do not show an excess of enthusiasm, at least at the beginning. You should not suddenly fly up to a colleague and happily slap him on the shoulder so that he spills coffee on the keyboard and completely spoils the mood. If you are a slow and drowsy person by nature, then you need to cheer up in time so as not to get on other's nerves. And believe me, there are ways to deal with the problem of drowsiness.

You only need to conduct a detailed analysis of your communication tools. Remember, we talked about observing, mirroring and establishing rapport? Maybe eight in the morning is not the best time to present your ideas to the boss. It may be better to make an appointment after dinner when your partner is more inclined to talk. If this is not possible, try to adjust to the rhythm of the person you are talking to. Otherwise, you and your ideas will meet not the warmest welcome.

SPOTTING INSECURITY

The indications of frailty point to the reality you never have a sense of safety. Unreliable individuals never have a sense of security, acknowledged, or OK. It incurs significant damage.

Few out of every odd uncertain individual gives indications of weakness the equivalent. What is frailty? It is actually what it implies. There will never be the point at which you have a sense of security, genuine, or secure in your very own skin. The most serious issue with being uncertain is that it doesn't generally seemed to be what it is. It is frequently misconstrued by the individuals around somebody uncertain.

Why? Since nobody needs to concede they live in dread of pretty much everything, that sounds insane. Thus, most uncertain individuals attempt to veil their nervousness, and spread it up with constant practices that don't work. They accomplish things that get them the careful inverse of what they hunger for—affection and acknowledgment.

20 indications of instability to watch out for

In the event that you wonder on the off chance that you are with somebody unreliable, or in the event that you ask whether you are uncertain yourself, these are the indications of instability that can't be covered up.

#1 They stress over everything. Did I say everything? I mean the world. There is definitely not a solitary thing that somebody who is unreliable doesn't stress over. They stress over their subsequent stage since they aren't sure they will arrive on safe ground. They consistently feel like the subsequent stage is sand trap.

#2 They never have a sense of security or settled. An uncertain individual never feels like they are protected or settled in their own life or in their very own skin. Normally encounters in their past sustain the frailty. They live in a condition of impermanent and they never get settled in light of the fact that it could all be no more.

#3 They pose similar inquiries again and again, as though they can't acknowledge the appropriate response. Like a youngster, they ask you similar inquiries again and again and over. How you answer matters not, they won't acknowledge your answer except if it is negative. They absolutely never put stock in anybody since they anticipate the most exceedingly awful.

#4 They push you away and afterward pull you back in. Somebody who is shaky needs to pull you in. At that point when you get excessively close, they monstrosity out and push you away. Their very own dread of dismissal drives them to continually push the very individuals they need close, far away. At that point once you leave, they implore you back.

#5 They continually inquire as to whether you are distraught or what they have done. Weakness prompts them always inquiring as to whether they have planned something for make you distraught. Stressed that they will lose you in the event that they don't do what you need and how you need it, their stressed nature has no base.

#6 They reliably apologize regardless of whether there's no expression of remorse essential. Never certain about themselves or how they run over, somebody shaky consistently feels as though they have accomplished something incorrectly and aren't above saying 'sorry' regardless of whether they haven't done anything by any stretch of the imagination.

Just so nobody is irate or angry with them, they simply express sorry to learn anything they could've done.

#7 They tend to disrupt their connections. Individuals who are uncertain never feel commendable enough to be seeing someone, causes a consistent uneasiness and dread that they will be discovered and left behind.

That prompts overcompensations to things and pushing individuals away when they dread that things are going gravely to ensure themselves. That can get them the very outcome they endeavor to evade in a relationship.

#8 They feel like everybody despises them. Perhaps the greatest indication of instability is that uncertain individuals always feel like everybody despises them. They can't generally disclose to you why or put their finger on what the issue is. They simply feel like everybody detests them.

#9 They stress in the event that somebody is speaking seriously about them constantly. Shaky individuals stress continually that individuals talk over them despite their good faith. Not having any desire to be disdained by individuals throughout their life, their instability drives them to persistently scan for affirmation that individuals don't care for them and are castigating them. For the most part, when there is no premise.

#10 They leave each circumstance thinking about whether they irritated anybody or aggravated somebody. Individuals who are unreliable are tension baffled practically constantly. They stress on the off chance that they said something rotten and replay the occasions of each snapshot of their social communications with individuals.

#11 They don't feel great in a gathering, so they for the most part have one individual they stick to. Uncertain individuals seem like outgoing people since they as a rule shroud the instability and turn on the appeal.

However, they ordinarily prefer to have one individual to stick to that makes them progressively secure and genuine. Typically just having the option to have each dear companion in turn, their kinship is their wellbeing zone when out with others.

#12 They strike hard when harmed. Uncertain individuals are continually injured. Their emotions are routinely harmed, which leads them to strike out against somebody who damages them. For the beneficiary, it appears to be an all out eruption.

Yet, because of the measure of strife and dread going on in the uncertain individual's psyche, it resembles repetitive sound never stops. Only one more thing in a flash sets them over the edge.

#13 They attempt to dazzle you, yet feel like a fraud inside, which makes them an apprehensive wreck. Most uncertain individuals don't appear to be shaky until you become more acquainted with them. Truly adept at veiling the individual so frightful inside, they build up a hard external shell, which makes them feel like a fraud constantly.

#14 Being distant from everyone else is their most exceedingly terrible dread. For unreliable individuals, being without anyone else is about the most noticeably terrible thing they can envision. They need other individuals to make themselves feel like everything is ok and safe. On the off chance that they lose somebody near them, it is overpowering, particularly somebody they love.

#15 They ache for endorsement, yet won't acknowledge it at any rate. Somebody uncertain pines for acknowledgment and endorsement. In any event, when given to them, they don't accept or acknowledge it. Regardless of whether the very thing they want gazes them in the face, they will not see it.

#16 They characterize themselves by what other individuals consider them. Uncertain individuals let other individuals disclose to them who and what they are on the grounds that they aren't very certain for themselves what they are made of. Always hoping to satisfy others and increase their acknowledgment, on the off chance that somebody doesn't care for them, it endures a colossal shot to their confidence.

#17 When you are with them you nearly feel the stirring of tension. Unreliable individuals are only difficult to be near. You can't put your finger on it, however they once in a while sit, they infrequently quit talking, or they simply have an anxious nervousness that tails them any place they go.

#18 They tend to be a fussbudget. Unreliable individuals don't have confidence in themselves, so they return and re-try everything around multiple times. Despite everything it won't ever be correct.

#19 They are envious of your associations with other individuals. Unreliable individuals are very tenacious. When they make you their stone, they get extremely desirous when you connect with another person.

They need you next to them to feel like nothing is wrong with the world and secure. In the event that you aren't bolstering their spirit, it feels vacant. They need 100% of you.

#20 They go overboard to apparently basic things. Since they continually convey a rucksack of apprehension, the littlest thing appears to set them off for reasons unknown. Persistent uneasiness is a troublesome thing to live with and can have somebody hitting the verge out of the blue and now and again making a mountain out of a molehill.

CONCLUSION

Be consistent in your words and non-verbal cues.

Speaking with another person, we influence him, whether we like it or not. Sometimes we do it intentionally, for example, when we are trying to piss off or cheer someone. Statements requiring a reaction may be as follows:

"You heard that ...", or

"This nasty Mel Gibson!", or

"You know what happened ?!", or

"I love you".

With our own statements, we can unconsciously cause a person to a variety of associations and reactions. For example, asking "How are you?" We never know what the answer will be. A person can take and pour out all his grief.

Our mood can also affect others. If we are happy, then everyone around us is also happy. We are sad—and others are sad too. Often we ask people to change:

"Get a hold of yourself!"

"Take it easy!"

In order to act more strongly, one must simultaneously with words produce actions convincing the interlocutor of the seriousness of your intentions. If you want to calm someone down, you should not take him by the shoulders and shake with a cry "When will you finally calm down?". To do this, you must first calm down yourself. Parents of babies understand how hard it is, but even with children, it works. "You must be tired," is the way to speak, accompanying the words with a yawn.

In this case, you need to radiate peace of mind, speak quietly, make smooth body movements, breathe evenly. To give someone confidence, you need to act confidently. Acting this way, you give the interlocutor's mind a hint, an example: you show with your appearance that it is possible to attain the desired state. There is a mutual understanding on a personal level. When you talk about something, you analyze; when you act, you create impressions, sometimes very strong. Think for yourself: would you prefer to talk about a kiss or get a kiss?

If your words mean one thing, and body language and voice mean another, the person will prefer to listen to the non-verbal message. If someone shouts "Calm down!", You will not listen to the words, but to the feelings that this cry will cause. It is unlikely that you calm down, rather, on the contrary, you get into a little more nervousness. To do this, do not even need to be able to read minds.

CPSIA information can be obtained
at www.ICGtesting.com
Printed in the USA
BVHW090927200122
626629BV00014B/1688